THE 8X8 COOKBOOK

THE 8X8 COOKBOOK

SQUARE MEALS FOR WEEKNIGHT FAMILY DINNERS, DESSERTS AND MORE—IN ONE PERFECT 8X8-INCH DISH

KATHY STRAHS

BURNT CHEESE
PRESS

Burnt Cheese Press | Los Gatos, California

Burnt Cheese Press
www.burntcheesepress.com

Design by Lorna Nakell, Interrobang Collective

Pyrex is a registered trademark of Corning Incorporated under license to World Kitchen, LLC.

ISBN: 978-0-9969112-0-7

Printed in the USA
First Edition

10 9 8 7 6 5 4 3 2 1

TABLE OF CONTENTS

INTRODUCTION

"I'm doing forks!!!"

If there's one chore I can easily get my kids to help with it's setting the table for dinner. They know there's usually good food on the way. Even if the meal is not one hundred percent to their liking—my kids aren't especially picky, but at 5- and 7 years old, certain vegetables are still approached with suspicion—they know that I cooked it for them with love.

Whether I'm making a meal for my family, hosting a dinner party for our friends, or creating recipes to share in my cookbooks or on my blogs, cooking is my expression of love and creativity. We all lead such busy lives these days—I actively look for ways to make mealtime something that's not only attainable, both in my house and in yours, but also highly enjoyable. Bringing a delicious dish out of the oven to set on the table and feed the ones you love—it doesn't get much better than that.

When I first began telling friends that I wanted to write a whole book about cooking with a "brownie pan" their response was unanimous—do it! They too appreciated how perfect that small square size was, whether they were feeding their family of four or six, or bringing food to share at a potluck or other gathering. Yet it wasn't always easy to find recipes for the 8x8-inch dish. Often, they had to take a larger recipe for a 9x13-inch dish and reduce the quantities by half to fit the smaller square—it works, but wouldn't it be nice to have a collection of dishes that were created with the needs of the 8x8 size in mind?

One afternoon, I opened up a Notes file on my phone and my husband Mike and I brainstormed all of the possible dishes we could think of that could be prepared in an 8x8 dish. We came up with dozens of family-friendly, yet company-worthy concepts within a matter of minutes—lasagnas and frittatas, roasted chicken and Thanksgiving sides, and—of course—brownies, cakes, and bars. Over the course of the next year, we added more and more ideas to the list. I started baking off a few here and there and it quickly became clear that not only would an 8x8 cookbook be incredibly useful and appreciated by many cooks at home; it also would be very tasty to write.

I learned to cook the way a lot of us do—by watching my mother in the kitchen. She made breakfast, lunch, and dinner for our family nearly every day—my favorites included pancakes and bacon on the weekends, lunch meat sandwiches in my Scooby Doo school lunchbox, Stuffed Shells (like the ones on page 49), and, of course, her signature chocolate chip cookies. She often let me pick recipes out of my children's cookbook to try and, while the dishes weren't exactly memorable, I was enormously proud that I could put a meal (of sorts) on the table. I came to appreciate cooking as both a life skill and an art form.

When I first started food blogging in early 2008, I couldn't have predicted that what started as a hobby would turn into a career for me. The more time I spent in the kitchen and interacting with other cooking enthusiasts, the more I wanted to learn about the ingredients I was using, taste new cuisines, and refine my techniques. Three blogs and two cookbooks later, I continue on my journey into exploring food and sharing the fruits of my exploration with others.

Whether you're looking for hands-off weeknight dinners to prepare for a busy family, impressive sides to serve at your next holiday gathering, or crowd-pleasing treats to offer at an upcoming bake sale, this book has you squarely covered. Many of the recipes are drawn from dishes that my family has enjoyed for years—and a number of them come from dishes that friends' parents and grandparents have passed down. It is my sincere hope that you find lots of new recipes that will become go-to favorites in your own homes for many years to come.

Share Food. Share Love.

For Mike, Hayley, and Cameron

—Love you more!

GLASS, CERAMIC AND METAL—OH MY!

There are a variety of choices when it comes to 8x8-inch dishes and pans—how do you decide which one to use? It all depends on what you're planning to bake and how you're planning to serve it. Here is a quick overview of the different types of dishes and pans, with my advice for choosing the right one for your needs.

G GLASS

Glass dishes are highly versatile, and often economical (many can be found for less than $15). I especially love the kitschy appeal of vintage milk glass Pyrex dishes—I find them online on Etsy and eBay, as well as in antiques and secondhand stores.

They're ideal for casseroles, as glass retains heat well and will keep your food warm once it's out of the oven for longer than metal pans will. Glass won't react to the acidity in foods, so it's a good choice for baked pastas and other tomato-based dishes. On the downside, food doesn't brown on the bottom as evenly in glass, so it's not my first choice for roasting. Also, glass shouldn't be used for high-temperature baking (450° F or above) as it may shatter.

C CERAMIC

Glazed ceramic bakers not only retain heat exceptionally well, they also come in a variety of colors and are perfect for transferring dishes directly from the oven to your dining table. They make delicious food look even more presentation-worthy, so they're my favorite dishes to use for the holidays and entertaining. Just as with glass, ceramic bakers won't transfer flavor to the food. Some high-quality ceramics, such as Le Creuset, can be used at high temperatures, and under the broiler.

M METAL

For cakes and roasts, I turn to my metal pan for its great heat conduction and browning capabilities. You can often find basic nonstick metal pans right in your local grocery store, but the pans sold at specialty cookware stores like Williams-Sonoma and Sur La Table are only a few dollars more and tend to be sturdier. Aluminum pans will react to acidic foods like tomatoes and lemons, imparting a metallic taste, so leave your baked pastas and other tomato-based dishes to the glass and ceramic bakers. (NOTE: In this book, I've written the instructions for metal pans based on how *light-colored* aluminum pans perform. If you're using a *dark metal* pan it will hold more heat and bake food faster—as a general rule, reduce the temperature by 25° F.)

HOW TO LINE A DISH WITH PARCHMENT

Lining your 8x8 dish or pan with baking parchment not only allows you to neatly lift out cakes, bars, breads, and other baked items, but it also means easier cleanup. You can buy rolls of parchment in your regular grocery store alongside the foils and plastic wraps.

1. Spray the bottom and sides of the dish or pan with cooking spray, or grease it with oil (this will act as an adhesive to keep the parchment in place).

2. Tear off a piece of parchment that's slightly larger than the width of your dish or pan (for an 8x8-inch dish, you'll want a sheet that's about 9 inches wide).

3. Press the paper into the dish or pan, allowing the excess to hang over the sides.

Now you're ready to lift out your baked items with ease!

NOTE: Always check the parchment package for the temperature limit—in general, it's recommended for use below 450° F, as it can burn at higher temperatures.

WEEKNIGHTS WON

HONEY-GLAZED CHICKEN WITH ROOT VEGETABLES

The shiny glazed chicken drumsticks get all the attention in this dish, but the roasted root vegetables relaxing beneath them really deserve some notice. Carrots, turnips, and potatoes are flavorful in their own right, and here, with honey-balsamic glaze traveling down from the chicken they become truly next level! They go into the oven partially cooked to make sure they're done right in synch with the chicken.

 Makes 4 Servings

INGREDIENTS:

1 cup roughly chopped carrots (about 2 medium)

1 cup roughly chopped turnips (1 to 2 small)

1 cup roughly chopped skin-on red potatoes (about ½ pound)

½ small red onion, cut into wedges

2 tablespoons honey

1 tablespoon balsamic vinegar

1 teaspoon ground thyme

¾ teaspoon coarse salt

½ teaspoon ground black pepper

2 tablespoons extra-virgin olive oil

1½ pounds chicken drumsticks

DIRECTIONS:

1. **Heat the oven to 400° F.**

2. Place the carrots, turnips, and potatoes in a microwave-safe bowl, cover with plastic wrap, and microwave on high for 4 minutes (alternatively, you can blanch the vegetables in a large pot of boiling water for 3 minutes). Drain any excess water and transfer the vegetables to an 8x8-inch glass or ceramic baking dish or metal baking pan. Add the onion wedges to the dish or pan.

3. In a small bowl, stir together the honey and balsamic vinegar. Set aside.

4. In a small bowl, combine the thyme, salt and pepper. Measure out ¾ teaspoon of the seasoning mixture and sprinkle it all over the vegetables. Drizzle olive oil over the vegetables and toss to combine.

Continued on next page

HONEY-GLAZED CHICKEN WITH
ROOT VEGETABLES—*continued*

5. Season the chicken with the remaining seasoning mixture—be sure to slide some of the seasonings under the skin as well as on the outside. Arrange the chicken on top of the vegetables. Roast for 20 minutes. Brush the chicken with half of the honey-balsamic mixture and roast for another 15 minutes. Brush the chicken with the remaining honey-balsamic mixture and continue roasting until the chicken reaches an internal temperature of 165° F and the vegetables are tender, about 10 minutes more (tent the chicken with foil if the glaze starts to burn).

SHORTCUT CHICKEN ENCHILADAS

While I cook primarily from scratch, I can appreciate a good cooking shortcut—especially when it's 5 o'clock on a Tuesday and my children begin to swarm the kitchen in search of dinner. These shortcut enchiladas have become one of my family's favorite weeknight dinners. Rotisserie chicken and store-bought sauce (I try to choose a good-quality one without preservatives) make it possible to have them out of the oven and on the table in under an hour.

 **Makes 6 servings**

INGREDIENTS:

Quick Pickled Onions:

1 red onion, halved and thinly sliced
½ cup apple cider vinegar
1 tablespoon brown sugar
1 teaspoon coarse salt
¼ teaspoon allspice

Enchiladas:

3 cups cooked chicken, shredded
1 cup (about 4 ounces) shredded
   Monterey Jack cheese
2 cups enchilada sauce,
   store-bought or homemade
6 (7-inch) corn tortillas
Fresh cilantro, chopped, for garnish

DIRECTIONS:

1. **Heat the oven to 400° F.**

2. Bring a small pot of water to a boil over high heat. Add the onions, bring the water back to a boil, and let the onions cook for about 15 seconds (this will take away some of the onions' "bite"). Drain the onions and set them aside. In a large nonreactive bowl, stir the vinegar, brown sugar, salt, and allspice until the sugar is dissolved. Add the onion slices and stir to coat them thoroughly in vinegar and seasonings. Cover the bowl and refrigerate the pickles while you prepare the enchiladas.*

Continued on next page

SHORTCUT CHICKEN ENCHILADAS
—continued

3. In a large bowl, combine the chicken and half of the cheese. Pour ½ cup of the enchilada sauce into an 8x8-inch glass or ceramic baking dish. Wrap the tortillas in a clean damp towel and microwave them on high for 30 seconds to make them roll more easily. Add about ½ cup of the chicken and cheese mixture to the center of a tortilla, roll it up and place it seam side down in the baking dish. Repeat for the remaining 5 tortillas. Pour the remaining 1½ cups enchilada sauce over the top and sprinkle with the remaining cheese.

4. Bake until the cheese is melted and lightly browned, 20 to 25 minutes. Serve topped with pickled onions and chopped cilantro.

*The pickles should stay fresh, refrigerated in an airtight container, for about 3 weeks.

TOP 8 MAKE AND TAKES

What makes a dish potluck-friendly? For me, it's all about ease of sharing and crowd-pleasing flavors. These 8x8 dishes are destined to be a hit at your next event—I doubt you'll bring home any leftovers!

1. Hot Ham and Cheese Sliders (page 27)

2. Tuna Melt Stuffed Mushrooms (page 42)

3. Roasted Shrimp, Tomato and Feta Bruschetta (page 44)

4. Layered Spinach, Artichoke and Crab Dip (page 98)

5. Corn Pudding (page 97)

6. Bacon, Spinach and Gruyère Crustless Quiche (page 109)

7. Triple Chocolate Saucepan Brownies (page 127)

8. Pumpkin Cheesecake Swirl Blondies (page 129)

TIP: When I travel with hot dishes, I use an insulated carrier like the *Rachael Ray Stowaway Potlucker* or *Lasagna Lugger*, with a heating pack. The food stays warm from my house to the event, so I don't have to reheat it once I arrive.

BAKED ORECCHIETTE WITH CHICKEN AND BROCCOLI

The simple goodness of this baked pasta is what I love most about it. All it takes are real ingredients and great flavor. Ear-shaped pasta and broccoli florets are ideal for cradling a savory Parmesan sauce. Shredding rotisserie chicken from the grocery store is an easy way to add protein and makes this a true "square" comfort meal.

 Makes 8 servings

INGREDIENTS:

- 8 ounces orecchiette or other short pasta
- 1 broccoli crown, chopped into florets
- 2½ cups whole milk
- 3 tablespoons unsalted butter, divided
- 1 tablespoon minced shallots
- 2 tablespoons all-purpose flour

- 1 cup (about 4 ounces) grated Parmesan cheese
- ½ teaspoon coarse salt
- ¼ teaspoon coarsely ground black pepper
- 2 cups shredded cooked chicken
- ¼ cup dry bread crumbs

DIRECTIONS:

1. **Heat the oven to 400° F.**

2. Grease an 8x8-inch glass or ceramic baking dish or metal baking pan with butter or cooking spray.

3. Boil the orecchiette according to the package directions. Three minutes before al dente, add the broccoli. Drain and set aside.

4. Heat the milk in a microwave-safe measuring cup or bowl in the microwave on high for 1 to 2 minutes, or in a small saucepan on the stove, until it's hot, but not boiling.

Continued on next page

BAKED ORECCHIETTE WITH CHICKEN AND BROCCOLI—*continued*

5. In a medium saucepan melt 2 tablespoons of the butter. Add in the shallots and cook, stirring occasionally, for about a minute until they're fragrant. Add the flour and whisk for about a minute until the flour is cooked and has a slightly nutty aroma, but is not yet browned. Gradually pour in the hot milk and bring the mixture to a boil, whisking constantly. Continue to whisk the sauce for 1 more minute, then remove it from the heat. Stir in the Parmesan cheese, salt and pepper until the cheese is fully incorporated. Stir in the cooked pasta, broccoli and chicken. Transfer the mixture to the prepared dish or pan.

6. Melt the remaining 1 tablespoon of butter in a microwave-safe bowl in the microwave on high for 45 to 60 seconds, or in a small saucepan over medium heat. Stir in the bread crumbs until they're coated well with butter. Sprinkle the bread crumbs over the pasta mixture.

7. Bake until the sauce is bubbly and the bread crumbs are browned, 20 to 25 minutes.

3B CHICKEN (BRINED, BREADED AND BAKED)

Oven-fried chicken is often viewed as a "next best" alternative to traditional fried chicken, but once you try this version I know you'll crave it specifically. Brining the chicken makes it extra flavorful throughout, and a savory bread crumb breading with a wee bit of butter in the mix ensures a crispy golden finish. I prefer to cook bone-in thighs because, to me, they have the most flavor and are the hardest to overcook, but you can take this same approach with any pieces you like, adjusting the baking time accordingly.

 Makes 4 servings

INGREDIENTS:

Chicken:

4 bone-in, skin on chicken thighs (about 1½ pounds)

Breading:

½ cup all-purpose flour
2 large eggs
¾ cup dry bread crumbs
2 tablespoons unsalted butter, melted
1 tablespoon chopped fresh thyme
½ teaspoon coarse salt
¼ teaspoon freshly ground black pepper
¼ teaspoon onion powder
¼ teaspoon paprika

Brine:

4 cups cold water
3 tablespoons coarse salt
1 tablespoon soy sauce
1 tablespoon sugar

Continued on next page

3B CHICKEN (BRINED, BREADED AND BAKED)—*continued*

DIRECTIONS:

1. In a large bowl, stir all of the brine ingredients together until the salt and sugar has dissolved. Place the chicken thighs in the brine, cover the bowl, and refrigerate for at least 1½ and no more than 3 hours (it will become too salty).

2. **Heat the oven to 400° F.**

3. Grease an 8x8-inch glass or ceramic baking dish or metal baking pan with oil or cooking spray.

4. Set up a dredging station: Add the flour to one shallow bowl. Add the eggs to another shallow bowl and whisk them well. Add the rest of the breading ingredients to a third shallow bowl, and mix them until well combined.

5. One at a time, remove a chicken thigh, rinse it in cold water, and pat it dry with paper towels. Dip the chicken first in the flour, then the eggs, then the bread crumb mixture, coating well each time. Arrange the breaded chicken pieces in the prepared dish.

6. Bake until the chicken is golden brown and cooked through to an internal temperature of 165° F, about 40 minutes.

ARROZ CON POLLO

"Cut a good size onion real fine..."—that's how the *arroz con pollo* recipe my friend Kelly shared with me begins. It's actually more of an account of how her Cuban grandmother makes this dish, jotted down by her aunt while observing her in action.

I adapted this classic Latin comfort meal, which Kelly's MiMa prepares on the stove, to fit an 8x8 dish and bake in the oven. The beer may be a surprising ingredient, but I'm told it's a must and it really does add an appealing tangy flavor to the rice. This is comfort food at its best.

 **Makes 6 servings**

INGREDIENTS:

1 tablespoon vegetable oil
1½ pounds chicken thighs and/or drumsticks
½ teaspoon coarse salt
¼ teaspoon freshly ground black pepper
1 cup chopped yellow onion
½ cup chopped green bell pepper
1 clove garlic, minced

1 teaspoon cumin
½ cup beer, such as a pilsner
½ cup low-sodium chicken broth
½ cup canned tomato sauce
1 teaspoon coarse salt
Pinch saffron
1 cup short-grain rice, such as bomba or Valencia*

DIRECTIONS:

1. **Heat the oven to 375° F.**

2. Heat the oil in a large skillet over medium-high heat. Season the chicken with salt and pepper. Brown the chicken on both sides, then transfer the chicken to a plate.

3. Add the onion, bell pepper, garlic, and cumin to the pan and cook, stirring occasionally, until the vegetables are softened, about 5 minutes. Meanwhile, in a small saucepan, bring the beer, chicken broth, tomato sauce, salt, and 1 cup of water to a simmer.

Continued on next page

ARROZ CON POLLO
—continued

4. Stir a good pinch of saffron into the vegetable mixture and cook for another minute. Add in the rice and stir until all of the rice is coated in oil. Transfer the rice mixture to an 8x8-inch glass or ceramic baking dish, spreading it in an even layer. Carefully pour the broth mixture over the rice. Arrange the chicken on top. Cover the dish tightly with foil.

5. Bake, covered, for 30 minutes. Taste a bit of the rice for doneness—set the dish back in the oven for a few more minutes if necessary.

[
*I'm not always able to find bomba or Valencia rice in my regular grocery store, but it's worth it to seek it out for this recipe. Specialty stores like Sur La Table typically carry it. A good alternative is Calrose rice—it's a short-grain rice that's often used for sushi, but works well in this dish too.
]

TURKEY-STUFFED ZUCCHINI

"Where's the pizza?", my son inquired when he popped into the kitchen the first time I made these stuffed zucchinis. The tomato sauce and mozzarella had his nose fooled. Its aromas may be reminiscent of a cheesy pizza or saucy baked pasta, but with lean turkey and no crust or pasta it's actually healthier (and, for those who need to avoid it, naturally gluten-free). Let your taste buds be fooled too!

 Makes 4 servings

INGREDIENTS:

1 tablespoon vegetable oil

2 cloves garlic, minced

½ pound ground turkey

½ teaspoon coarse salt

¼ teaspoon freshly ground
   black pepper

2 medium zucchini

½ cup (about 2 ounces) grated
   Parmesan cheese

3 cups marinara sauce, divided

½ cup (about 2 ounces) shredded
   mozzarella cheese

DIRECTIONS:

1. **Heat the oven to 400° F.**

2. Grease an 8x8-inch glass or ceramic baking dish with oil or cooking spray.

3. Heat the oil and garlic in a large skillet over medium heat. Add the ground turkey, salt and pepper and cook, breaking up the turkey into crumbles and stirring occasionally, until it's browned, 8 to 10 minutes. Set aside.

4. Trim the ends of the zucchini, and slice each in half lengthwise to create four halves. Use a spoon to scoop out the flesh of the zucchini, leaving a ¼-inch border around the edge. Arrange the zucchini halves side-by-side in the prepared baking dish.

Continued on next page

5. Chop up the scooped-out zucchini flesh and add it to the skillet with the browned turkey. Stir in the Parmesan cheese and 1 cup of marinara sauce. Divide the mixture among scooped-out zucchini halves—it doesn't need to fit precisely. Pour the remaining 2 cups of marinara over the top of the turkey mixture and top with the mozzarella cheese. Cover the dish tightly with foil.

6. Bake, covered, for 30 minutes. Remove the foil and continue baking until the zucchini is tender, the sauce is bubbly, and the cheese is lightly browned, another 10 to 15 minutes.

LET'S DISH ABOUT VINTAGE PYREX

We must have wandered in and out of 20 antiques stores on the row before we struck gold—or, I should say, glass. There was a big sign out front that said "WE SPECIALIZE IN PYREX." Eureka!

That sunny spring afternoon my friend, Meilee, and I had driven out to the historic Niles shopping district in Fremont, California in search of kitschy, colorful vintage Pyrex 8x8-inch baking dishes to use in the photography for this book. Corning Glass Works introduced their opal glass line in the 1940s and produced them until the 1980s—hence the retro-chic styling. I can remember many pieces in our kitchen cabinets growing up, and at my grandma's house. Now I've got them in mine!

Pyrex was designed to be both beautiful and useful. Food releases from the glass like a dream, and the dishes hold heat really well, which is great when you want food to stay warm for a while outside the oven.

I came home from Niles that day with a lime green 222 series dish (the 8-inch square) for $15. Later that evening I logged onto Etsy and eBay and discovered the bakers were a bit more plentiful online, albeit with a small shipping charge. Within minutes, I had the "flamingo pink" and "butterfly gold" dishes on their way to my doorstep. Since then, I've picked up three more solid color Pyrex 222's ("gold" and "avocado"), another patterned one ("crazy daisy"), and a regular 8-inch clear dish. What can I say? I am in Pyrex love.

PAN ROASTED PORK CHOPS WITH APPLES AND COUSCOUS

If I were to pan roast pork chops in the traditional way, I'd first brown them in a skillet on the stove and then transfer the skillet to the oven to finish cooking. They would be juicy and delicious... but I'd be lacking other components of the meal. By finishing in a baking dish, rather than a skillet, I still get juicy chops *plus* I have the chance to fill the bottom of the dish with couscous, load the top with apples and onions, and cook the entire meal at once. Flavors are shared, mouths are happy.

G C M **Makes 4 servings**

INGREDIENTS:

2 tablespoons unsalted butter

4 (½-inch thick) boneless pork chops, about 1⅓ pounds

1½ teaspoons coarse salt, divided

½ teaspoon freshly ground black pepper

1 yellow onion, halved and thinly sliced

1 sweet apple, peeled, cored, and thinly sliced

1 cup uncooked couscous

¾ cup apple cider

1 teaspoon Dijon mustard

¼ teaspoon ground cinnamon

¼ teaspoon dried thyme

DIRECTIONS:

1. **Heat the oven to 400° F.**

2. Melt the butter in a large skillet over medium high heat. Season the pork chops on both sides with 1¼ teaspoons of the salt and the pepper. Brown the pork on both sides, 3 to 4 minutes per side. Transfer the pork to a plate and set aside.

3. Turn the heat down to medium and add the onions and apples to the skillet. Cook, stirring occasionally, until they're tender, 8 to 10 minutes.

4. Add the couscous to an 8x8-inch glass or ceramic baking dish or metal baking pan.

Continued on next page

PAN ROASTED PORK CHOPS WITH APPLES AND COUSCOUS—*continued*

5. Pour the cider and ½ cup of water into a small saucepan. Whisk in the mustard until it's dissolved. Add the cinnamon, thyme, and the remaining ¼ teaspoon salt and bring the mixture to a boil—watch it carefully so it doesn't boil over!

6. Immediately pour the boiling hot cider mixture over the couscous. Arrange the browned pork chops on top, and add the cooked onions and apples over the pork. Cover the dish tightly with foil.

7. Bake until the couscous has absorbed all of the liquid and the pork is cooked through to an internal temperature of 145° F, 15 to 18 minutes. Fluff the couscous with a fork a bit before serving.

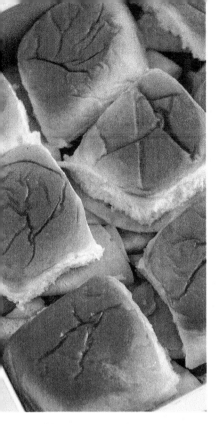

HOT HAM AND CHEESE SLIDERS

I know I've got a winner when my 5-year-old shouts "I want that!" when he spies a dish I've pulled out of the oven. Little hot sandwiches like these are a weeknight treat to my kids—and I can always switch up what goes inside. Here, I've gone with classic ham and cheese on sweet Hawaiian rolls, with a pickle-and-yellow mustard nod to my favorite Cuban sandwiches.

G C M **Makes 9 sliders (about 4 servings)**

INGREDIENTS:

9 Hawaiian rolls, split lengthwise

9 small slices Swiss cheese

3 tablespoons yellow mustard

18 dill pickle slices

9 slices deli ham

1 tablespoon unsalted butter, melted

HERE'S A TIP: Put the "wet" ingredients like mustard and pickles on the inside so the bread doesn't get soggy.

DIRECTIONS:

1. **Heat the oven to 350° F.**

2. In an 8x8-inch glass or ceramic baking dish or metal baking pan, arrange the bottom halves of the Hawaiian rolls in three rows. Assemble the sandwiches by layering on the cheese, mustard, pickles, and ham. Close the sandwiches with the top halves of the rolls, and brush butter on each top.

3. Bake the sandwiches until the cheese is melted, 10 to 15 minutes.

BAKED TORTELLINI ALFREDO WITH PANCETTA, PEAS AND LEMON

It may not take much effort to pull this baked pasta together, but you'd never know it by its flavors. Fresh lemon zest, sweet peas, and crispy pancetta elevate store-bought tortellini in Alfredo sauce to something crave worthy. The uncooked pasta simmers right in the baking dish—no need to boil it first. I can find a spot on the couch, grab a magazine and just *lounge* in the half hour or so that this dish takes to bake. That's a win to me!

G C M **Makes 6 servings**

INGREDIENTS:

1 (20 ounce) package uncooked fresh cheese tortellini*

1 cup fresh or frozen peas

2 teaspoons finely grated lemon zest

1 (15 ounce) jar Alfredo sauce, regular or reduced fat

2 ounces diced pancetta

1 cup (about 4 ounces) grated Parmesan cheese

Fresh pasta is my preferred choice for this recipe, but if you decide to use dried tortellini you'll need to bake it for longer.

DIRECTIONS:

1. **Heat the oven to 400° F.**

2. Place the tortellini, peas, and lemon zest in an 8x8-inch glass or ceramic baking dish or metal baking pan.

3. Whisk together the Alfredo sauce with 2 cups of water in a large measuring cup or medium bowl. Pour the sauce mixture all over the ingredients in the baking dish and stir to combine. Cover the dish tightly with foil.

Continued on next page

4. Bake until the tortellini is tender, about 35 minutes. While the tortellini bakes, cook the pancetta in a large skillet over medium heat, stirring occasionally, until it's crisp. Transfer the pancetta to a paper towel-lined plate to drain.

5. Once the tortellini is tender, remove the foil, stir in the crisped pancetta, and sprinkle the Parmesan cheese all over the top of the dish. Cover the dish again and bake until the cheese is melted, about 10 minutes more.

HAM, CHEDDAR AND POLENTA BAKE

Even after ham sandwiches, ham omelets, and straight picking ham off of the bone, I am always left looking for ways to use up our leftover holiday ham. One Easter, the idea for this dish came to me—a comfort food casserole I could make in under an hour for dinner, and would be equally welcome for breakfast the next morning as well.

You'll want to get all of your ingredients chopped and grated before you start because once the polenta is hot and ready, you need to work quickly to get it mixed and poured into the baking dish before it firms up.

 Makes 9 servings

INGREDIENTS:

2 cups whole milk

1½ cups quick-cooking polenta

1 teaspoon coarse salt

1½ cups (about 6 ounces) shredded sharp cheddar cheese, divided

4 large eggs

2 cups diced cooked ham

1 cup chopped scallions

2 teaspoons chopped fresh rosemary

¼ teaspoon coarsely ground black pepper

⅛ teaspoon ground cayenne pepper

DIRECTIONS:

1. **Heat the oven to 425° F.**

2. Grease an 8x8-inch glass or ceramic baking dish with butter or cooking spray.

3. In a large saucepan over medium-high heat, bring the milk and 2½ cups water to a simmer. Reduce the heat to medium-low and gently stir in the polenta and salt. Simmer, stirring frequently, until it's thickened, 5 to 7 minutes. Be careful—as the polenta starts to cook it may bubble up, so lower your heat as needed. Remove the pan from the heat and stir in 1 cup of the cheese until it melts completely.

Continued on next page

4. Separately, beat the eggs in a small bowl. Add about ¼ cup of the polenta mixture to the eggs and whisk briskly to heat up the eggs. Pour the warmed eggs into the polenta mixture and mix until thoroughly combined. Mix in the ham, scallions, rosemary, pepper, and cayenne.

5. Pour the polenta mixture into the prepared dish, spreading it to the edges and smoothing the top. Sprinkle on the remaining cheese. Bake until the casserole is set and the top is lightly browned, 30 to 35 minutes.

SALAMI AND MOZZARELLA STUFFED CHICKEN BREASTS

Chicken Cordon Bleu, *involtini di pollo*, *roulade de poulet*... no matter what you want to call them, stuffed chicken breasts are always a fun switch from "plain old chicken" for dinner. I love this Italian-style version—with salami, mozzarella, and fresh basil on the inside and crunchy herbed bread crumbs on the outside—but you can stuff the chicken with whatever meats, vegetables, or cheeses you happen to have on hand. Serve these chicken breasts with a big green salad, sautéed vegetables, or even over a bed of spaghetti with marinara for inside-out chicken *parmigiana*!

G C M **Makes 4 servings**

INGREDIENTS:

1 tablespoon unsalted butter
⅔ cup panko bread crumbs
1 teaspoon dried basil
½ teaspoon coarse salt
½ teaspoon dried thyme
½ teaspoon garlic powder
¼ teaspoon freshly ground
   black pepper

2 egg whites
2 boneless, skinless chicken breasts,
   1 to 1½ pounds
4 ounces low-moisture mozzarella
   cheese, thinly sliced
8 slices salami
4 to 8 fresh basil leaves

DIRECTIONS:

1. **Heat the oven to 350° F.**

2. Grease an 8x8-inch glass, ceramic or metal baking dish with oil or cooking spray.

3. Heat the butter in a large skillet over medium heat. Add the panko bread crumbs and stir to coat them in butter. Continue cooking, stirring frequently, until the bread crumbs are golden brown, 4 to 5 minutes. Remove the pan from the heat and stir in the dried basil, salt, dried thyme, garlic powder, and pepper. Transfer the mixture to a shallow bowl.

Continued on next page

4. In another shallow bowl, whisk the egg whites until they turn a bit foamy, about 1 minute.

5. With a sharp knife, carefully split the chicken breasts horizontally (parallel to the cutting board) to create 4 thin cutlets.* Lay a sheet of plastic wrap over the cutlets and pound them, with a mallet, until they're ¼-inch thick. Discard the plastic wrap. On each cutlet, layer on cheese, salami, and basil leaves— enough to thinly cover most of each cutlet. Starting at the narrowest end, carefully roll up each cutlet.

6. One at a time, dredge each rolled cutlet first in the egg whites (keep your fingers on the seam to hold it closed), then in the panko mixture. Press the panko onto the chicken to help it adhere. Transfer the chicken, seam side down, to the prepared dish.

7. Bake until the chicken is cooked through to an internal temperature of 165° F, 30 to 40 minutes.

*You can always ask your butcher to cut the chicken breasts for you.

SEASONING SYNERGIES: Notice we don't season the chicken directly in this recipe? That's because the salami and mozzarella, when it's rolled up with the chicken, provides plenty of salty flavor. If you opt to substitute less salty ingredients, such as roasted red peppers or spinach, you'll want to season the chicken with ½- to 1 teaspoon of salt.

ITALIAN HERB BAKED MEATBALLS

Taking the time to make homemade meatballs during the week feels a little luxurious, but they actually come together really quickly. While the meatballs are in the oven, there's just enough time to boil pasta, prepare mashed potatoes, roast some vegetables, or throw together a salad.

G C M **Makes 4 to 6 servings**

INGREDIENTS:

½ pound ground beef
  (85% lean/15% fat)
½ pound ground pork
1 large egg, lightly beaten
½ cup dry bread crumbs
¼ cup (about 1 ounce) grated Parmesan
  cheese

1 clove garlic, minced
1 teaspoon dried Italian salt-free
  seasoning*
1 teaspoon coarse salt
½ teaspoon freshly ground black pepper
Pinch cayenne pepper

Alternatively, use ¼ teaspoon each of dried basil, oregano, rosemary, and thyme.

Continued on next page

DIRECTIONS:

1. **Heat the oven to 425° F.**

2. Grease an 8x8-inch glass or ceramic baking dish or metal baking pan with oil or cooking spray.

3. Mix all of the ingredients in a large bowl (it's easiest to use your clean hands for this one) just until they're combined, being careful not to overwork the meat (which can make the meatballs dense and less tender). Divide the meat mixture into 16 equal portions and, in the palms of your hands, roll them into balls. Arrange the meatballs in the prepared pan, four rows of four meatballs each.

4. Bake the meatballs until they're browned and an instant-read thermometer measures 160° F, 15 to 20 minutes.

ROASTED COD WITH GREMOLATA AND LEMONY ORZO

Here's an all-in-one weeknight dinner that also makes a really nice lunch for a group of friends. Steaming the fish over a bed of par cooked orzo keeps it moist and flaky, while the pasta gets just enough moisture to get to al dente. Gremolata—a simple condiment comprised of parsley, lemon zest, garlic, and olive oil—brings a punch of zesty flavor that pairs perfectly with the fish.

 Makes 4 servings

INGREDIENTS:

Fish:

4 (½-inch thick) fresh cod filets or frozen, thawed (about 1 pound)
¾ teaspoon coarse salt
¼ teaspoon freshly ground black pepper

Orzo:

2 strips lemon zest
1 tablespoon coarse salt
1 cup orzo
1 tablespoon extra-virgin olive oil

Gremolata:

2 tablespoons chopped fresh parsley
1 tablespoon extra-virgin olive oil
2 teaspoons freshly squeezed lemon juice
1 teaspoon grated lemon zest
1 clove garlic, minced

DIRECTIONS:

1. **Heat the oven to 400° F.**

2. Bring a medium pot of water to boil with the lemon zest strips. Add the salt and orzo and boil the orzo for 8 minutes—it won't be quite done yet; it'll finish cooking in the oven. Reserve ¼ cup of the pasta water, then drain the orzo in a colander. Discard the lemon zest strips. Transfer the orzo to an 8x8-inch glass or ceramic baking dish and toss it with the olive oil to coat.

Continued on next page

3. Mix all of the gremolata ingredients together in a small bowl.

4. Season the cod filets on both sides with salt and pepper.

5. Pour the reserved pasta water over the orzo in the baking dish. Arrange the cod filets on top. Spoon the gremolata over each of the filets. Cover the dish tightly with foil.

6. Bake until the fish is cooked through and opaque and the orzo is al dente, 15 to 20 minutes.

SMOKED SALMON, SPINACH AND HERBED GOAT CHEESE PHYLLO PIE

I received an enthusiastic email from my friend Cyndy, raving about the "outrageously delicious" smoked fish quiche she'd just eaten at a restaurant in LA (my friends know I will share in their joy over these things). I couldn't get the thought of these flavors in pie form out of my head for the rest of the weekend. That Monday, I created this phyllo-wrapped pie, with bright pink hot smoked salmon as the star. Chopped spinach and tangy herbed goat cheese surround the salmon, making a wonderfully flavorful light dinner. I can't say for sure how it compared with Cyndy's quiche, but I was thrilled with the results.

The best part about a rustic pie like this is that imperfections give it character. The more ruffled and haphazard the flaky, tissue-thin phyllo layers are, the prettier they look.

 Makes 4 to 6 servings

You want to use hot smoked salmon for this dish, which is cooked and flaky. Save the silky, moist cold smoked salmon for bagels and crostini.

INGREDIENTS:

5 ounces goat cheese, at room temperature
1 tablespoon chopped fresh dill
1 tablespoon chopped fresh chives
1 tablespoon chopped fresh parsley
4 sheets frozen phyllo dough, thawed
¼ cup extra-virgin olive oil
2 (4-ounce) hot smoked salmon filets, skin removed*
2 cups chopped frozen spinach, thawed and drained

Continued on next page

SMOKED SALMON, SPINACH AND HERBED GOAT CHEESE PHYLLO PIE—*continued*

DIRECTIONS:

1. **Heat the oven to 400° F.**

2. Line an 8x8-inch glass or ceramic baking dish or metal baking pan with parchment (see page 3 for a tutorial).

3. In a mixing bowl, beat the goat cheese, dill, chives, and parsley with an electric mixer on high speed until it's fluffy and well combined.

4. Stack two full sheets of phyllo on a clean surface, keeping the remaining sheets covered with plastic and a damp towel to prevent them from drying out. Cut the sheets in half with kitchen shears or a sharp knife, creating two smaller rectangles. Working carefully, lay one rectangle in the prepared dish or pan, horizontally, allowing the excess dough to hang over the sides. Brush the dough, including the overhang, all over with olive oil. Rotate the dish or pan a quarter-turn and lay down the next rectangle, horizontally. Brush the dough all over with olive oil. Repeat for the remaining two rectangles (no need to brush the last rectangle with oil).

5. Spread the goat cheese in an even layer on top of the phyllo. It doesn't need to be perfectly smooth—you just want relatively even coverage. Flake the salmon with a fork and distribute it in an even layer over the goat cheese.

6. In batches, roll the spinach in a clean towel, twist the ends and wring the towel repeatedly to remove as much moisture as possible. Scatter the spinach all over the salmon (including between and around the filets, if you kept them intact).

Continued on next page

7. Stack the remaining 2 full sheets of phyllo on a clean surface, and cut them in half with kitchen shears or a sharp knife. Layer the 4 phyllo rectangles, brushing each with olive oil and rotating the dish or pan just as before. Carefully fold the overhang pieces toward the center in a rustic, decorative way—there's no need to try to make them lay perfectly flat, the more "imperfect" and ruffled the layers are, the prettier the pie will look once baked. Be sure that all the phyllo has been brushed with olive oil to ensure even browning.

8. Bake until the phyllo is golden brown and flaky, 17 to 20 minutes. Allow the pie to cool for 10 minutes, then lift it out by the parchment and cut it into squares to serve.

TUNA MELT STUFFED MUSHROOMS

Like many 5-year-olds, my son has a penchant for swiftly dropping grocery items into my shopping cart when I'm not looking. But there is occasionally an oddball amidst the goldfish crackers, Oreos, and random plastic toys he procures: portobello mushrooms. My little guy happens to love them.

One day, when the mushrooms stealthily appeared in the shopping cart, I came up with the idea for this simple dinner recipe to use them. I had everything for tuna melts on hand—they're something that *I* happen to love—and baby portobello caps made the perfect little serving receptacle for them.

G C M **Makes 4 to 6 servings**

INGREDIENTS:

9 baby portobello or large crimini mushrooms, about 2½-inch diameter, cleaned and scraped

2 (5 ounce) cans albacore, drained

¼ cup finely chopped celery (1 to 2 ribs)

¼ cup finely chopped onion (¼ medium onion)

¼ cup mayonnaise, regular or reduced fat

½ teaspoon coarse salt

¼ teaspoon freshly ground black pepper

9 thin tomato slices (about 2 medium tomatoes)

1 cup (about 4 ounces) shredded sharp cheddar cheese

MUSHROOM CLEANING 101: Wipe the cap of each mushroom with a damp paper towel to remove any dirt. Twist off the stem (you can save it for another use or discard it). One at a time, cradle a mushroom cap in one hand and, with a small spoon in the other hand, gently scrape out all of the gills from inside the cap. Don't worry if you accidently tear the sides a little—just press it all back together when it's time to stuff them.

Continued on next page

DIRECTIONS:

1. **Heat the oven to 425° F.**

2. Grease an 8x8-inch glass or ceramic baking dish or metal baking pan with oil or cooking spray.

3. Arrange the cleaned and scraped mushrooms, cap side down, in the prepared dish or pan.

4. Mix the tuna, celery, onion, mayonnaise, salt and pepper in a medium bowl until well combined. Fill each mushroom with the tuna mixture. Top each mushroom with a tomato slice and a few tablespoons of cheese (it's okay if you mound the cheese a little, it will flatten as it melts).

5. Bake until the cheese is melted and lightly browned on top, 20 to 25 minutes.

ROASTED SHRIMP, TOMATO AND FETA BRUSCHETTA

Don't you sometimes wish you had a nice hunk of bread to dip in the tasty juices left in the pan? Well, your wish is granted with this dinner bruschetta. The shrimp and tomatoes are roasted right on top of a bed of crusty bread, soaking up all of the goodness.

 Makes 4 servings

INGREDIENTS:

3 tablespoons extra-virgin olive oil, divided

4 to 6 (½-inch thick) slices ciabatta or other rustic bread

1 pound medium-sized shrimp, peeled, deveined, tails removed

1 pound Roma tomatoes, sliced into wedges

3 tablespoons chopped fresh parsley

2 cloves garlic, minced

2 teaspoons freshly squeezed lemon juice

¾ teaspoon coarse salt

¼ teaspoon freshly ground black pepper

2 ounces crumbled feta cheese

DIRECTIONS:

1. **Heat the oven to 400° F.**

2. Drizzle 1 tablespoon of olive oil in an 8x8-inch glass or ceramic baking dish, and swirl the dish to coat the bottom. Arrange bread slices inside the dish—the exact number of slices needed will vary according to the size of your bread, but you want to try and cover most of the bottom.

Continued on next page

3. In a large nonreactive bowl, toss together the shrimp, tomatoes, parsley, the remaining 2 tablespoons olive oil, garlic, lemon juice, salt, and pepper. Pour the shrimp mixture over the bread in the baking dish—don't worry about making anything fit precisely on individual bread slices, just pour it all on top. Scatter the feta cheese on top.

4. Bake until the shrimp is pink and cooked through, about 20 minutes.

KNIFE AND FORK IT: Unlike traditional handheld bruschetta, you're going to want utensils for this one!

MY BEST MACARONI AND CHEESE

My kids would eat macaroni and cheese for every meal, every day if I let them. Blue box or homemade, they're not particular—but my good old-fashioned baked mac and cheese casserole is definitely their favorite. I've played around with the cheeses over the years, and I've found I prefer a combination of sharp cheddar for its tangy flavor, and fontina or Gruyère for their meltability and stretchiness. Smoked and cured country ham is a real treat to add in here—the salty, smoky flavor permeates throughout the casserole—but our family loves this dish just as much in its "pure" cheesy form.

 Makes 6 to 8 servings

INGREDIENTS:

- ½ pound (8 ounces) cavatappi, elbow macaroni, or other short pasta
- 2½ cups whole milk
- 3 tablespoons unsalted butter, divided
- ¼ cup all-purpose flour
- 1½ cups (about 6 ounces) shredded sharp cheddar cheese
- 1½ cups (about 6 ounces) shredded fontina or Gruyère cheese
- ¾ cup diced country ham, optional
- 1 teaspoon Dijon mustard
- 1 teaspoon coarse salt
- ⅛ teaspoon freshly ground black pepper
- ⅛ teaspoon freshly grated nutmeg
- ¾ cup panko bread crumbs

DIRECTIONS:

1. **Heat the oven to 400° F.**

2. Grease an 8x8-inch glass or ceramic baking dish or metal baking pan with butter or cooking spray.

3. Bring a large pot of water to a boil. Add the pasta and cook, stirring occasionally, for two minutes less than the package recommends for al dente (you'll finish cooking it in the oven). Drain the pasta in a colander.

Continued on next page

4. Meanwhile, make the cheese sauce. Heat the milk, either in the microwave or in a small saucepan on the stove, until it's hot but not boiling. In a medium saucepan, melt 2 tablespoons of butter over medium heat. Whisk in the flour to form a thick paste and cook, whisking occasionally, until the aroma of the mixture is more nutty than floury, 2 to 3 minutes. Gradually pour in the hot milk and bring the mixture to a boil, whisking constantly. The sauce will be thicker at this point. Continue to whisk the sauce for 1 more minute, then remove it from the heat. Stir in 1 cup of each cheese, ham (if using), mustard, salt, pepper, and nutmeg until the cheese sauce is fully combined. Stir in the cooked pasta.

5. Pour the mixture into the prepared baking dish or pan. Sprinkle the remaining cheese all over the top. Melt the remaining 1 tablespoon of butter in a small microwave-safe bowl in the microwave, then mix in the panko and stir to combine. Sprinkle an even layer of the panko topping over the casserole. Bake, uncovered, until the cheese sauce is bubbling and the panko topping is browned, 20 to 25 minutes.

SAUSAGE AND SPINACH STUFFED SHELLS

Jumbo stuffed pasta shells, brimming with sausage, cheese, and marinara sauce, were part of my mom's regular dinner rotation when I was growing up, and they always ranked among our favorites. These days, I add spinach to the mix to get in some healthy greens and they're still a hit with my kids. Clocking in at close to an hour, they take a bit longer to complete than many of my weeknight dinners. But on evenings when you can spare the time, the smiles on their faces will be well worth it.

G C M **Makes 6 to 8 servings**

INGREDIENTS:

- ½ (12-ounce) package (about 6 ounces) jumbo shell pasta
- ½ pound bulk Italian sausage
- 1 tablespoon extra-virgin olive oil
- 6 ounces chopped fresh baby spinach, or frozen, thawed and drained
- ½ cup finely chopped yellow onion
- 1 clove garlic, minced
- ½ teaspoon coarse salt
- ⅛ teaspoon freshly ground black pepper
- Pinch nutmeg
- 1 large egg
- 1 cup (about 4 ounces) part-skim ricotta cheese
- ¼ cup (about 1 ounce) grated Parmesan cheese
- 2 cups marinara sauce
- ½ cup (about 2 ounces) shredded low-moisture mozzarella cheese

DIRECTIONS:

1. **Heat the oven to 350° F.**

2. Cook the jumbo shells in a large pot of boiling salted water according to the package directions. Drain the pasta in a colander, reserving 2 tablespoons of the pasta water. Set aside.

Continued on next page

SAVE SOME FOR LATER: If you wind up with more filled shells than will fit in your baking dish, wrap them up tightly and keep them in the freezer to bake another day. Your future self will thank you!

3. While the shells are cooking, brown the sausage, breaking it up with your spoon and stirring occasionally, in a large skillet over medium heat until it's no longer pink, 7 to 10 minutes. Drain the excess grease. Add the olive oil, spinach (if you're using frozen spinach, be sure to wring out the extra moisture in a clean towel first), onion, garlic, and reserved pasta water to the skillet. Continue cooking, stirring occasionally, until the onions are softened and the spinach is wilted, about 10 minutes. Remove from the heat and stir in the salt, pepper and nutmeg. Set aside.

4. In a large bowl, mix the egg, ricotta, and Parmesan cheese until well combined. Mix in the sausage mixture.

5. Spread ½ cup of the marinara sauce inside the bottom of an 8x8-inch glass or ceramic baking dish.

6. Fill approximately 20 cooked jumbo shells with a few spoonfuls of the sausage-cheese mixture—enough to be full, but not overstuffed. Place each filled shell in the baking dish. Pour the remaining marinara sauce over the shells, and sprinkle the mozzarella cheese all over the top. Cover the dish tightly with foil.

7. Bake, covered, until the cheese is melted and the sauce is bubbly, about 30 minutes.

PASTA FRITTATA

You don't have to wait until you have leftover pasta on hand to make this frittata—although if you do, it's one of the best ways I know to use it. Long strands of spaghetti or angel hair pasta look especially pretty strewn throughout this dish, but shorter cuts like penne will also work well. Who doesn't love a good breakfast-for-dinner?

 Makes 4 to 6 servings

INGREDIENTS:

1 can (14.5 ounce) no-salt added diced tomatoes

½ pound cooked pasta

1 cup (about 4 ounces) low-moisture mozzarella cheese, cubed

4 large eggs

4 ounces goat cheese, at room temperature

½ cup (about 2 ounces) grated Parmesan cheese, divided

½ teaspoon dried basil

½ teaspoon coarse salt

¼ teaspoon dried thyme

¼ teaspoon freshly ground black pepper

DIRECTIONS:

1. **Heat the oven to 400° F.**

2. Grease an 8x8-inch glass or ceramic baking dish with oil or cooking spray.

3. Drain the tomatoes and toss them with the pasta and mozzarella in a large bowl; transfer the mixture to the prepared baking dish. In a medium bowl, beat the eggs with the goat cheese, ¼ cup of the Parmesan cheese, dried basil, salt, dried thyme, and pepper. Pour the egg mixture over the pasta in the baking dish. Sprinkle the remaining ¼ cup of Parmesan on top.

4. Bake the frittata until the eggs are set and the cheese is lightly browned, about 30 minutes. Serve warm or at room temperature.

CHUNKY RATATOUILLE GOAT CHEESE PASTA

When summer hits and your garden (or, in my case, farmers market or grocery store) is brimming with fresh zucchini, tomatoes, and eggplant, you'll want to reach for this simple, fresh recipe, inspired by the classic Provencal *ratatouille* vegetable dish. Soft goat cheese, mixed in at the end, creates its own tangy, creamy sauce for the pasta.

 Makes 4 to 6 servings

INGREDIENTS:

1 (6 to 8 ounces) Japanese eggplant, cut into 1-inch pieces

1 (6 ounce) zucchini, cut into 1-inch pieces

6 ounces cherry tomatoes

½ small red onion, cut into 1-inch pieces

2 tablespoons extra-virgin olive oil

¾ teaspoon coarse salt

¼ teaspoon freshly ground black pepper

½ pound rigatoni or other short pasta

4 ounces goat cheese, at room temperature

2 tablespoons chopped fresh basil

DIRECTIONS:

1. **Heat the oven to 425° F.**

2. Line an 8x8-inch metal baking pan with parchment (see page 3 for a tutorial).

3. Place the eggplant, zucchini, tomatoes, and onions in a large bowl. Toss with the olive oil, salt, and pepper to coat. Pour the vegetable mixture into the prepared pan and roast, stirring occasionally, until the tomatoes are blistered and the vegetables are cooked through and beginning to brown, 30 to 35 minutes.

Continued on next page

CHUNKY RATATOUILLE GOAT CHEESE PASTA—*continued*

4. Meanwhile, boil the pasta to al dente in salted water according to the package directions. Drain, reserving 2 tablespoons of the pasta water.

5. When the vegetables are done, add the cooked pasta, reserved pasta water, and 2 ounces of goat cheese to the baking pan (alternatively, you can transfer it all to a separate serving dish). Toss to coat. Dot the remaining goat cheese over the top and garnish with basil.

KALE, MUSHROOM AND ONION GRATIN

When I notice my 7-year-old daughter dragging the edge of her fork across her plate, in an effort to capture every last bit of sauce, that's a pretty good indicator to me that I nailed the dish. The creamy Asiago Mornay sauce in this comforting vegetarian main is truly worth some fork dragging, and its slightly sharp, nutty flavor complements the kale, mushrooms and onions perfectly. The crunchy bread crumb topping makes the dish a *gratin*, a "gourmet" sounding name for an otherwise simple combination of fresh ingredients.

 Makes 6 to 8 servings

INGREDIENTS:

5 tablespoons unsalted butter, divided, plus more for greasing the dish

6 cups chopped kale (1 to 2 bunches, stems removed)

1 cup sliced yellow onion (about 1 medium onion)

8 ounces crimini mushrooms, washed and sliced

¾ teaspoon coarse salt, divided

2 cups whole milk

2 cloves garlic, minced

2 tablespoons all-purpose flour

1 cup (about 4 ounces) grated Asiago cheese, divided

¼ teaspoon freshly ground black pepper

⅛ teaspoon freshly grated nutmeg

⅔ cup panko bread crumbs

Continued on next page

KALE, MUSHROOM AND ONION GRATIN
—*continued*

DIRECTIONS:

1. **Heat the oven to 400° F.**

2. Grease an 8x8-inch glass or ceramic baking dish with butter or cooking spray.

3. Melt 2 tablespoons of butter in a large skillet over medium-high heat. Add the kale, onions, mushrooms, and ½ teaspoon of salt. Cook the vegetables, stirring occasionally, until the kale is wilted, the onions are softened, the mushrooms are tender, and most of the liquid in the pan has evaporated, 10 to 12 minutes.

4. Meanwhile, heat the milk in the microwave on high for 2 minutes, or in a small saucepan over medium-low heat. The milk should be hot but not boiling.

5. Melt another 2 tablespoons of butter in a medium saucepan over medium heat. Add the garlic and cook until fragrant, about 30 seconds. Whisk in the flour to form a thick paste and cook, whisking occasionally, until the aroma of the mixture is more nutty than floury, 2 to 3 minutes. Gradually pour in the hot milk and bring the mixture to a boil, whisking constantly. The sauce will be thicker at this point. Continue to whisk the sauce for 1 more minute, then remove it from the heat. Whisk in half of the Asiago cheese, the remaining ¼ teaspoon of salt, pepper, and nutmeg until smooth. Stir in the cooked vegetables until well combined. Pour the vegetable mixture into the prepared baking dish. Sprinkle the remaining cheese on top.

6. Melt the remaining 1 tablespoon of butter in a medium microwave-safe bowl in the microwave on high for 30 to 60 seconds (or in a small saucepan over medium heat on the stove). Add the panko and stir until the bread crumbs are well coated in butter. Sprinkle the buttered panko all over the top of the mixture in the dish.

7. Bake until the sauce is bubbly and the bread crumb topping is golden brown, 13 to 17 minutes.

SUNDAY DINNER TABLE

ROSEMARY ROASTED GAME HEN WITH GRAPES FOR TWO

In old movies, they used to show couples out on a romantic date night, seated at a fancy restaurant table with a white tablecloth, taper candles, and one of those big covered silver platters between them. A tuxedoed waiter would lift off the cover to reveal a glistening, roasted chicken. It's the gold standard for romantic dinners—and yet, in reality, a whole roasted chicken provides much more than those hungry couples in the movies could have possibly eaten. A Cornish game hen, however, is the perfect petite size for two. Roast grapes with rosemary, olive oil, and balsamic vinegar to accompany it for a sweet evening in with someone special.

 Makes 2 servings

INGREDIENTS:

Grapes:

¾ pound seedless grapes, one color or assorted, stems attached
1 tablespoon extra-virgin olive oil
1 tablespoon balsamic vinegar
½ teaspoon chopped fresh rosemary
¼ teaspoon coarse salt
⅛ teaspoon freshly ground black pepper

Game Hen:

1 (1½ to 2 pounds) Cornish game hen, fully thawed if frozen
2 sprigs fresh rosemary, plus ¼ teaspoon chopped leaves
1 teaspoon extra-virgin olive oil
½ teaspoon coarse salt
⅛ teaspoon freshly ground black pepper

Continued on next page

ROSEMARY ROASTED GAME HEN WITH GRAPES FOR TWO—*continued*

DIRECTIONS:

1. **Heat the oven to 450° F.**

2. Gently toss the grape ingredients together in a large bowl. Set aside.

3. Pat the hen dry with paper towels. Stick the rosemary sprigs into the cavity and tie the legs with kitchen twine. Set the hen inside an 8x8-inch glass or ceramic baking dish, breast side up. Tuck the tips of the wings under the hen. Rub olive oil all over the hen and season it with salt and pepper. Sprinkle the chopped rosemary leaves on top. Arrange the grapes and any excess oil and vinegar from the bowl around the hen.

4. Bake until the skin on the hen is browned and crispy and an instant-read thermometer inserted at the thigh measures 165° F, 40 to 45 minutes.

CURRIED CHICKEN POT PIE

Get ready for this comforting, not-too-spicy twist on a chicken pot pie. Inspired by the balti pies that football (aka soccer) fans enjoy in the UK, I've topped a tangy tomato-based chicken curry with flaky, golden puff pastry. To get those deep, complex flavors it does require quite a few ingredients but if you take care of all chopping, dicing, and mincing at the outset you'll be surprised by how easily this impressive dish comes together.

 Makes 6 servings

INGREDIENTS:

2 tablespoons unsalted butter
1½ pounds boneless skinless chicken
    thighs, cut into bite-sized pieces
2 tablespoons curry powder
2 teaspoons coarse salt, divided
1 cup peeled and diced yellow potatoes
    (about ½ pound)
½ cup diced carrots (1 to 2 medium)
1 cup diced yellow onion, (about
    1 small)
2 cloves garlic, minced
1 tablespoon ground cumin
1 tablespoon brown sugar

1 teaspoon garam masala
1 teaspoon ground coriander
½ teaspoon ground ginger
Pinch cayenne pepper
¼ cup all-purpose flour
2 cups low-sodium chicken broth
1 (14.5-ounce) can no-salt added
    diced tomatoes, drained
1 teaspoon tomato paste
1 sheet puff pastry (from a 17¼-oz
    package), thawed
1 large egg

YOU CAN FIND IT: The spices are what really "make" this dish, and they should be relatively easy to find in most major grocery stores.

Continued on next page

CURRIED CHICKEN POT PIE
—continued

DIRECTIONS:

1. **Heat the oven to 375° F.**

2. Melt the butter in a large (12-inch) skillet or Dutch oven over medium heat. Add the chicken, sprinkle the curry powder and 1 teaspoon of salt over the top, and cook, stirring occasionally, until the chicken is cooked through, 8 to 10 minutes.

3. While the chicken is cooking, place the potatoes and carrots in a micro-wave-safe bowl with 2 tablespoons of water. Cover the dish with a lid or plastic wrap and microwave on high for 5 minutes, until the vegetables are cooked and soft. Set aside.

4. Once the chicken is done, transfer it to a plate and set aside. Add the onions to the skillet or Dutch oven and cook, stirring occasionally, until they're soft-ened, about 5 minutes. Add the garlic, cumin, brown sugar, garam masala, coriander, ginger, and cayenne pepper. Cook and stir for another minute. Sprinkle the flour over the top of the onion mixture and stir to coat. Stir in the chicken broth, tomatoes, and tomato paste. Bring to a simmer and continue simmering for 5 minutes to allow the mixture to thicken. Stir in the cooked chicken, potatoes, carrots, and the remaining teaspoon of salt. Pour the mix-ture into an 8x8-inch glass or ceramic baking dish.

5. On a lightly floured surface, roll out the puff pastry to a 10x10-inch square. Cover the baking dish with the puff pastry, pressing it lightly around the out-side of the dish. Cut slits in the puff pastry to allow steam to vent. In a small bowl, whisk the egg with a splash of water to make an egg wash. Brush the egg wash all over the surface of the puff pastry.

6. Set the dish on the center rack, and a rimmed baking sheet on a lower rack to catch any sauce that may bubble over. Bake until the puff pastry is puffed and golden brown, 30 to 35 minutes.

GREEK-STYLE SAUSAGE AND PEPPERS

When friends from other countries share their traditions with me—particularly those I can eat—I feel so fortunate. My friend Eleni, an investment adviser and mom of two adorable little girls, was born and raised in Greece and has a wealth of amazing Greek recipes. She is the one who first introduced me to *spetzofai*—a Greek sausage and peppers dish, simmered in a zesty tomato-based sauce. It's traditionally a spicy dish, made with spicy sausages or peppers, but I dial down the heat for my family by choosing milder ones. Be sure to make a big pot of rice to soak up these incredible fresh flavors.

 Makes 4 to 6 servings

INGREDIENTS:

3 cups cubed eggplant (about ½ large or 1 to 2 Japanese)

1 teaspoon coarse salt

4 tablespoons extra-virgin olive oil, divided

¾ pound fully-cooked pork or chicken smoked sausages, sliced

1 small yellow onion, sliced

1 green bell pepper, cored and sliced

1 red bell pepper, cored and sliced

2 cloves garlic, minced

1 tablespoon tomato paste

½ teaspoon dried oregano

2 cups diced tomatoes (about 2 to 3 medium)

¼ teaspoon sugar

¼ teaspoon freshly ground black pepper

DIRECTIONS:

1. **Heat the oven to 400° F.**

2. Toss the eggplant with salt in a colander. Set the colander over a bowl to catch any moisture that is drawn out from the eggplant for at least 30 minutes. In the meantime, prepare the other ingredients.

Continued on next page

3. Heat 1 tablespoon olive oil in a large skillet over medium high heat. Add the sausage slices and brown them on both sides, about 4 to 5 minutes. With tongs or a slotted spoon, transfer the sausages to a paper towel-lined plate—keep the remaining oil in the pan.

4. Reduce the heat to medium. Add the onions and peppers to the same skillet and cook them, stirring occasionally, until they're tender, 8 to 10 minutes. Transfer the vegetables to an 8x8-inch glass or ceramic baking dish.

5. Add 2 tablespoons of olive oil and the eggplant to the skillet. Cook the eggplant, stirring occasionally, until it's browned, 5 to 7 minutes. Transfer the eggplant to the baking dish.

6. Add the remaining tablespoon of olive oil, garlic, and tomato paste to the skillet, and cook until the garlic is fragrant, about 30 seconds. Stir in the tomatoes, 1 cup of water, oregano, sugar, and pepper, scraping up any browned bits from the bottom of the skillet. Bring the mixture to a boil.

7. Pour the tomato mixture into the baking dish. Add in the sausages and carefully stir to combine—the dish will be quite full. Cover the dish tightly with aluminum foil.

8. Bake for 30 minutes to allow sauce to simmer and flavors to combine. Serve over rice or with crusty bread.

KNOW YOUR SKILLET: I've written this recipe so that you can prepare all of the components in a single skillet (a boon to dishwashers everywhere!). Plus, cooked on bits can really enhance the flavor of a dish. But burnt bits don't. Every pan is different and if you find that the residual bits in yours are starting to burn, by all means continue with a clean skillet (either wash the one you were using or pull out a new one).

PASTITSIO

Pastitsio is sometimes nicknamed "Greek mac and cheese" but, really, it's a unique dish all its own (and another Greek favorite from my friend Eleni—see also Greek-style Sausage and Peppers on page 66 and Mary's Best Baklava on page 160). Instead of mixing the cheese sauce in with the pasta, the sauce sits as a savory custard on top. A layer of ground beef, simmered with wine and tomatoes, runs between two layers of long, tubular pastitsio pasta. Ideally you want to wait a bit for the dish to cool before slicing so you can fully appreciate those luscious layers, both by taste and sight.

 Makes 6 to 8 servings

INGREDIENTS:

½ pound pastitsio,* bucatini, or
 penne pasta
1 tablespoon extra-virgin olive oil
½ pound ground beef (85%
 lean/15% fat)
1 cup diced yellow onion (about 1 small)
2 cloves garlic, minced

Béchamel:
4 tablespoons unsalted butter
¼ cup all-purpose flour
1 cup whole milk
1 large egg, lightly beaten
1 cup (about 4 ounces) grated
 Parmesan cheese

¾ teaspoon coarse salt, divided
¼ teaspoon freshly ground
 black pepper
¼ cup red wine
¼ cup chopped fresh parsley
1 cup no-salt added canned diced
 tomatoes, undrained

¾ teaspoon coarse salt
⅛ teaspoon freshly ground
 black pepper

Find pastitsio (aka pastichio) pasta, which is long and tubular, in international and specialty food stores or online, such as on Amazon.com. Bucatini or penne are suitable substitutes.

Continued on next page

PASTITSIO—*continued*

DIRECTIONS:

1. **Heat the oven to 375°F.**

2. Grease an 8x8-inch glass or ceramic baking dish with butter or cooking spray.

3. Boil the pasta in a large pot of salted water according to the package directions. Drain in a colander.

4. Meanwhile, heat the olive oil in a large skillet over medium heat. Add the ground beef, onion, garlic, ½ teaspoon salt, and pepper and cook, stirring occasionally, until the meat is browned. Add in the wine (and perhaps pour a glass for the cook!) and scrape up any of the bits stuck to the pan with your spoon. Stir in the tomatoes, parsley and another ¼ teaspoon salt, and let the mixture simmer until most of the liquid has evaporated. Remove from the heat and set aside.

5. Transfer half of the pasta to the prepared baking dish, spreading it an even layer all over the bottom of the dish. Next, spread the meat mixture in an even layer on top of the pasta. Finally, top the meat with an even layer of the remaining pasta.

6. To make the béchamel, melt the butter in a medium saucepan over medium heat. Whisk in the flour to form a thick paste and cook, whisking occasionally, until the aroma of the mixture is more nutty than floury, 1 to 2 minutes. Reduce the heat to medium-low and whisk in the milk, then the beaten egg. Mix in half of the Parmesan cheese, and the salt and pepper. Taste the sauce and adjust the seasoning if needed. The sauce should be somewhat thick, like a light custard.

7. Sprinkle the remaining Parmesan over the pasta in the baking dish. Top the Parmesan with the béchamel, spreading the sauce to the edges. The béchamel should form its own layer on top of the casserole.

8. Bake until the béchamel is set and browned on top, 45 to 50 minutes. The casserole will be easier to cut—and see those lovely layers—if you wait for it to cool a bit.

The 8x8 Cookbook

DETROIT-STYLE DEEP DISH PIZZA

I find myself letting out a grand exhale as I remove this glorious beast of a pizza from its pan. You might say it's a labor of love to make it but wow is it worth it. This deep dish is most akin to Detroit-style pies, which are typically square, with cheese to the edges and sauce on top. I included my family's favorite toppings here, but by all means, get creative and customize to your own personal taste.

 Makes 4 to 6 servings

INGREDIENTS:

Crust:

2 cups all-purpose or bread flour

1 teaspoon coarse salt

½ teaspoon instant yeast

2 tablespoons extra-virgin olive oil, divided

¾ cup water, at room temperature

Sauce:

1 (14.5 ounce) can no-salt added canned diced tomatoes*

1 clove garlic, minced

½ teaspoon coarse salt

1 teaspoon dried basil

½ teaspoon dried thyme

¼ teaspoon dried oregano

¼ teaspoon freshly ground black pepper

Toppings:

2 cups (about 8 ounces) shredded low-moisture mozzarella cheese

½ pound bulk Italian pork sausage

¼ cup sliced black olives

½ green bell pepper, sliced

*If you can't find no-salt added tomatoes, omit the salt in the sauce, taste it, and add more if needed.

[NOTE: This recipe requires an 8x8-inch metal baking pan without a nonstick coating. Due to the high heat required, do not use glass or ceramic dishes or a nonstick metal pan.]

Continued on next page

DETROIT-STYLE DEEP DISH PIZZA—*continued*

DIRECTIONS:

1. The night before, combine the flour, salt, yeast and 1 tablespoon of olive oil in a large bowl. Add in the water and mix with a wooden spoon until well combined. Knead the dough in the bowl for several minutes, until the dough comes together and becomes too sticky to handle. Cover the bowl with plastic wrap and let the dough rest at room temperature overnight (at least 8 hours, and up to 15 hours).

2. The next morning, add the remaining olive oil to an 8x8-inch metal baking pan (without a nonstick coating) and spread it all over the bottom and sides with your hands. Punch down the dough and transfer it to the baking pan. Turn the dough over once in the pan to coat it with oil. Cover the pan with plastic wrap and place it in the refrigerator.

Continued on next page

3. Ninety minutes before baking, take the dough out of the refrigerator and let it rise and spread at room temperature.

4. Thirty minutes before baking, make sure an oven rack is in the middle position and **heat the oven to 550°F.** Drain the tomatoes for the sauce in a colander—give them a good 20 minutes to drain all the excess water (this will keep your pizza from getting soggy!).

5. While the oven is heating and the tomatoes are draining, brown the sausage in a large skillet over medium heat until it's cooked through and no longer pink.

6. Once the tomatoes are drained, blend them with the garlic, salt, basil, thyme, oregano, and pepper in a food processor. Set the sauce aside.

7. Gently push and stretch the pizza dough into the corners of the baking pan, as well as up the sides if the dough allows. Sprinkle a handful of cheese on top of the dough. Add sausage. Sprinkle on the rest of the cheese, all the way to the edges (you'll be rewarded with irresistible crusty cheese on the sides). Add peppers and olives, then dollop the sauce on top—as much or as little as you'd like.

8. Bake until the cheese is melted, browned, and crusted around the edges, 15 to 20 minutes. Slide a thin knife around the edges of the pan to help release the crusty cheese, if needed, as you lift the pizza out of the pan.

SPINACH-PESTO LASAGNA

This has been my go-to lasagna for quite a while now, not just for my own family on any given Sunday but also as a great make-ahead dish for bringing to friends with new babies, or if I'm heading out of town and my husband needs something easy to pop in the oven. Sure, it's an indulgent cheesy dish—three types of cheese in fact!—but there's also a full pound of healthy spinach in there. They ought to counterbalance each other, right? Deliciously wishful thinking!

 Makes 6 servings

INGREDIENTS:

1 (14.5 ounce) can diced tomatoes

1½ cups (about 6 ounces) part-skim ricotta cheese

½ cup (about 2 ounces) grated Parmesan cheese

1 large egg

16 ounces frozen chopped spinach, thawed and squeezed dry

8 tablespoons basil pesto

6 no-boil lasagna noodles

1 cup (about 4 ounces) shredded low-moisture mozzarella cheese

DIRECTIONS:

1. **Heat the oven to 375°F.**

2. Drain the tomatoes in a colander for 20 minutes to remove most of the excess liquid.

3. In a large bowl, beat together the ricotta, Parmesan, and egg until well combined. Mix in the spinach.

Continued on next page

4. Spread 2 tablespoons of the pesto in the bottom of an 8x8-inch glass or ceramic baking dish. Layer on two lasagna noodles (side by side), ⅓ of the tomatoes, ⅓ of the spinach mixture (use your fingers to spread it to edges of the noodles—don't be afraid to get a little messy), 2 tablespoons of pesto (just dot it on with a spoon), and ⅓ of the mozzarella. Repeat the layers two more times. Spray a coating of cooking spray inside a sheet of foil, to keep the cheese from sticking, and cover the dish with the foil. If you're freezing the lasagna to bake later, you can freeze it at this point. Thaw it overnight in the refrigerator the night before you're ready to bake it.

5. Bake, covered, for 45 minutes—the lasagna noodles will expand as they cook. Remove the foil and bake until the cheese is bubbly and lightly browned, another 9 to 12 minutes.

STREAMLINE IT: This is a super-simple recipe, but there's some assembly required. To make things easiest, prepare all of your ingredients and line them up in small bowls. Then it's just a matter of making your way down the line to assemble the lasagna layers.

ZUCCHINI, CORN AND GREEN CHILE TAMALE PIE

I'm not a vegetarian but, like a lot of people these days, I try to go meatless a few days a week. The trouble is, when it comes to vegetarian mains, I often end up missing the meat. So I find a compromise in "vegetable forward" dishes where vegetables are the star, with meat in a supporting role. This tamale pie is a perfect example. It's all about fresh summer zucchini and corn and smoky-sweet green chiles. It would be completely vegetarian if I made the masa with vegetable shortening and vegetable broth, but the meat eater in me appreciates the savory flavor that lard and chicken broth bring to the tamale crust.

 Makes 8 servings

INGREDIENTS:

Masa:

2 cups masa harina*
2 cups low-sodium chicken or
   vegetable broth
½ cup cold lard*, vegetable shortening
   or butter
1 teaspoon baking powder
1 teaspoon coarse salt

Filling:

1 tablespoon vegetable oil
2 cloves garlic, minced
2 cup frozen corn kernels, thawed
2 zucchini, halved lengthwise and sliced
1 (4 ounce) can diced green chiles
½ teaspoon coarse salt
⅛ teaspoon freshly ground black pepper
½ cup salsa verde
4 ounces queso fresco

Look for masa harina in the baking or Latin foods sections of major grocery stores. Get rendered pork lard from your butcher or in Latin grocery stores—the tan-colored, refrigerated variety will provide the best flavor (with less saturated fat than butter, by the way!).

Continued on next page

DIRECTIONS:

1. **Heat the oven to 350° F.**

2. Grease an 8x8-inch glass or ceramic baking dish or metal baking pan with oil or cooking spray.

3. In a medium bowl, mix the masa harina and chicken broth until well combined.

4. In a large mixing bowl, beat the lard or shortening, baking powder, and salt with an electric mixer or by hand with a wooden spoon until it's lightly whipped and fluffy. Add in ⅓ of the masa harina mixture at a time, beating between each addition, until it's fully incorporated and has a soft, spongy texture. Set the bowl aside while you prepare the filling.

5. Heat the vegetable oil in a large skillet over medium heat. Add the garlic and cook for about 1 minute until it's fragrant. Add the corn, zucchini, chiles, salt, and pepper and cook, stirring frequently, until the zucchini is tender, about 10 minutes.

6. With wet fingers, gently press about ⅔ of the masa mixture into the bottom and edges of the prepared dish or pan. Add the vegetable mixture in an even layer. Spoon the salsa over the vegetables, and crumble the queso fresco over the salsa. Spoon on the remaining masa and, with wet fingers, spread it evenly across the top to form a top crust, and sealing the edges.

7. Bake until the masa is cooked through and lightly golden on top, about 1 hour 15 minutes.

ON THE SIDE

GREEK YOGURT AND HONEY CORNBREAD

Don't get me wrong, I love a good old-fashioned buttery cornbread. But when I discovered just how moist and cake-like a cornbread made with Greek yogurt in place of butter or oil could be, I began taking this lower-fat approach from time to time too. Honey gives this cornbread a hint of sweetness without any refined sugar. I won't judge if you still want to smear on a little butter when these squares come out of the oven (actually, I'll join you).

G C **Makes 9 servings**

INGREDIENTS:

1 cup cornmeal

1 cup all-purpose flour

1½ teaspoons baking powder

1 teaspoon coarse salt

½ teaspoon baking soda

1 cup whole milk

⅓ cup reduced-fat Greek yogurt

¼ cup honey

1 large egg

DIRECTIONS:

1. **Heat the oven to 375° F.**

2. Grease an 8x8-inch glass or ceramic baking dish with butter or baking spray. Alternatively, for metal pans, heat the oven to 400° F and prepare the pan in the same manner.

3. In a large bowl, whisk together the cornmeal, flour, baking powder, salt, and baking soda. In a small bowl, whisk together the milk, yogurt, honey, and egg. Add the wet ingredients to the dry ingredients and stir until combined. Pour the batter into the prepared baking dish or pan.

4. Bake until the cornbread is lightly browned on top and a toothpick inserted at the center comes out clean, 25 to 30 minutes.

CHARD APPLE STUFFING

If you're like me and stuffing is always your very favorite dish on the Thanksgiving table, you're in for a treat. This recipe encompasses everything I think a great stuffing should be—savory with just a little sweetness from autumn apples, bread that's soft on the inside but toasty and golden on the outside, and pretty to look at on the buffet. This just might become your family's new go-to!

G C M **Makes 6 to 8 servings**

INGREDIENTS:

5 tablespoons unsalted butter

1 cup diced yellow onion (about 1 small)

1 cup diced sweet apples, such as Gala (about 1 medium)

½ cup chopped celery (about 2 ribs)

¼ cup chopped fresh parsley

2 teaspoons chopped fresh sage, or ½ teaspoon dried

2 teaspoons chopped fresh thyme, or ½ teaspoon dried

¾ teaspoon coarse salt

¼ teaspoon freshly ground black pepper

4 cups coarsely chopped Swiss chard (about half of a 1-pound bunch), stems removed

5 cups day-old Italian bread, cut into 1-inch cubes (about a half-pound loaf)

2 large eggs, beaten

⅓ cup low-sodium chicken broth

DIRECTIONS:

1. **Heat the oven to 375° F.**

2. Grease an 8x8-inch glass or ceramic baking dish or metal baking pan with butter or cooking spray.

3. Melt the butter in a large skillet over medium heat. Add the onions, apples, celery, parsley, sage, thyme, salt, and pepper and cook, stirring occasionally, until the onions are softened, 6 to 8 minutes. Add the chard and continue cooking for another 3 minutes until the chard is wilted.

Continued on next page

4. Place the bread cubes in a large bowl, add the vegetable mixture and toss to combine. Mix in the beaten eggs and the broth; stir until well combined. Pour the stuffing into the prepared baking dish. Spray a piece of foil with cooking spray (or grease it with butter) and cover the dish, greased side down.

5. Bake for 30 minutes. Remove the foil and bake until the stuffing is golden, 15 to 20 minutes more.

TOP 8 FREEZE-AHEAD DISHES

Whether you like to cook ahead for your own family or you're helping to line a friend's freezer with meals (a lovely gesture when life's demands leave little time to cook), look to these freezable 8x8 recipes.

1. Baked Orecchiette with Chicken and Broccoli (page 13)

2. Cheesy Broccoli Casserole (page 95)

3. Italian Herb Baked Meatballs (page 34)

4. My Best Macaroni and Cheese (page 47)

5. Pastitsio (page 69)

6. Sausage and Spinach Stuffed Shells (page 49)

7. Shortcut Chicken Enchiladas (page 9)

8. Spinach-Pesto Lasagna (page 74)

Allow the dishes to cool completely, wrap individual portions tightly with plastic wrap or press-and-seal wrap, and seal the wrapped portions in plastic freezer bags (don't forget to label and date them!). These dishes will taste best if reheated within 6 months. Defrost individual portions as you need them in the refrigerator or in the microwave on the defrost setting.

ALL-HOMEMADE GREEN BEAN CASSEROLE

Our Thanksgiving menu evolves from year to year, but one dish that always makes the cut is the classic green bean casserole. It's the first casserole I ever learned to make on my own, in seventh grade home ec. We made it in the way that people have made casseroles for decades in America—a can of this, a can of that, bake 'til bubbly. You can't deny it's delicious.

These days, my green bean casserole is entirely homemade. Blanching fresh green beans not only preserves their fresh flavor, but also their vibrant green color. I don't need a canned soup because I can make an amazing savory mushroom gravy from scratch with no hassle. Store-bought fried onions are addictively delicious, but so are freshly fried shallots, with even more oniony flavor and without the extra salt. I'm all about this new-fashioned take on an old-fashioned favorite.

G C **Makes 6 to 8 servings**

INGREDIENTS:

Vegetable oil, for frying

2 shallots, thinly sliced

1 tablespoon plus 1 teaspoon coarse salt, divided

1 pound green beans, trimmed and cut into 2- to 3-inch pieces

2 tablespoons unsalted butter

1 cup (about 3 ounces) cleaned,* thinly sliced shiitake mushrooms

1 small onion, halved and thinly sliced

2 tablespoons all-purpose flour

1 cup low-sodium chicken broth

1 cup heavy cream

¼ teaspoon freshly ground black pepper

To clean shiitake mushrooms, start by wiping the dirt off each mushroom cap with a damp paper towel. Next, remove the tough stems by pinching them where they meet the cap and gently prying them off.

Continued on next page

DIRECTIONS:

1. **Heat the oven to 400° F.**

2. In a large skillet or Dutch oven, add enough oil to fill about ½-inch deep. Heat the oil over medium heat until shimmering. Add the shallots and cook, stirring frequently, until they're golden, 10 to 15 minutes. Using a slotted spoon, transfer the shallots to a paper towel-lined plate to drain.

3. Bring a large pot of water to a boil. Add 1 tablespoon of salt and the green beans, and cook the green beans for 5 minutes. Drain the beans in a colander and immediately transfer them to a large bowl of ice water to stop the cooking and preserve their color. Drain and set aside.

4. Melt the butter in a large skillet over medium heat. Add the mushrooms and onions and cook, stirring occasionally, until the mushrooms are tender and the onions are translucent, 10 to 12 minutes. Sprinkle flour over the mixture, stir to combine and cook for another minute. Add the broth and bring the mixture to a simmer. Continue simmering for 1 minute. Add in the cream and cook, stirring occasionally, until the mixture thickens, 6 to 8 minutes.

5. Remove the skillet from the heat and stir in the remaining teaspoon of salt and the pepper. Taste, and adjust the seasoning as necessary. Stir in the green beans and ¼ of the fried shallots. Pour the mixture into an 8x8-inch glass or ceramic baking dish.

6. Bake for 10 minutes. Add the remaining fried shallots on top and continue baking until the casserole is bubbly, about 5 minutes.

BALSAMIC GLAZED KALE SPROUTS WITH PANCETTA AND PARMESAN

If you haven't tried kale sprouts (aka Kalettes), hopefully this recipe will be the nudge you need to seek them out. A cross between Brussels sprouts and kale, they have the taste of both superfoods and look like teeny tiny heads of kale. They roast rather quickly and, tossed in a light, sweet glaze with pancetta and Parmesan, I find them irresistible.

 Makes 2 to 4 servings

INGREDIENTS:

½ pound kale sprouts*
¼ cup small-diced pancetta
1 tablespoon extra-virgin olive oil
¼ teaspoon coarse salt
⅛ teaspoon freshly ground
  black pepper

1 tablespoons honey
2 teaspoons balsamic vinegar
½ teaspoon Dijon mustard
Parmesan cheese, for shaving

DIRECTIONS:

1. **Heat the oven to 400° F.**

2. Toss the kale sprouts, pancetta, olive oil, salt, and pepper together in an 8x8-inch metal baking pan. Roast, stirring periodically, until the kale and pancetta are crisped, about 30 minutes.

3. In a small bowl, whisk together the honey, balsamic vinegar, and Dijon mustard. Pour the glaze over the kale sprouts and roast for another 5 minutes. Serve with Parmesan shaved on top.

Look for kale sprouts at specialty grocery stores like Trader Joe's and Whole Foods, or at your local farmers market. Alternatively, this recipe is also delicious with halved or quartered Brussels sprouts.

MAPLE BACON BAKED BEANS

Far be it from me to shy away from a dish that takes all day to prepare. I am game for it, and I know the results are usually well worth it. That said, if I can manage to make a version of that same dish that I love just as much but only takes a fraction of the time? Count me in. With these Maple Bacon Baked Beans, starting with plain canned beans lets me cut down on hours of soaking and simmering, while I still get all the rich homemade flavor.

G C **Makes 6 to 8 servings**

INGREDIENTS:

8 slices bacon, divided
1 tablespoon vegetable oil
1 yellow onion, finely chopped
½ cup ketchup
¼ cup firmly packed dark brown sugar
2 tablespoons maple syrup

1 tablespoon Worcestershire sauce
1 teaspoon Dijon mustard
½ teaspoon coarse salt
2 (16 ounce) cans navy or white beans, rinsed and drained

DIRECTIONS:

1. **Heat the oven to 375° F.**

2. Lay four whole slices of bacon in the bottom of an 8x8-inch glass or ceramic baking dish. Bake for 10 minutes to allow them to begin to crisp up. Meanwhile, heat the oil in a large skillet over medium heat. Cook the onions, stirring occasionally, until they are softened and translucent, 7 to 9 minutes.

3. In a medium bowl, mix the ketchup, brown sugar, maple syrup, Worcestershire sauce, mustard, and salt until well combined. Mix in the beans. Pour the mixture over the bacon in the baking dish, spreading in an even layer. Lay the remaining 4 slices of bacon on top. Cover tightly with foil.

4. Bake 30 minutes. Uncover, and continue baking until the bacon on top is crisped, 20 to 25 minutes more.

CARROT CUSTARD

"Can you pack this in my lunch?!" When my 5-year-old actually requests a dish full of vegetables, I know it tastes good. This custard reminds me a lot of pumpkin pie, not just because of the bright orange hue but the flavors of apple and cinnamon always evoke autumn and Thanksgiving. We enjoy it as a holiday side dish, but with a dollop of whipped cream on top it could easily be reinvented as dessert.

 **Makes 8 to 10 servings**

INGREDIENTS:

1 pound carrots, peeled and quartered
2 large eggs
½ cup sugar
1 cup all-purpose flour
¼ cup vegetable oil

¼ cup unsweetened applesauce*
2 cups whole milk
2 teaspoons vanilla extract
1 teaspoon ground cinnamon

Continued on next page

CARROT CUSTARD—*continued*

DIRECTIONS:

1. **Heat the oven to 325° F.**

2. Grease an 8x8-inch glass or ceramic baking dish with oil or cooking spray.

3. Place the carrots and 2 tablespoons of water in a microwave-safe bowl. Cover the bowl with a lid or plastic wrap and microwave it on high for 6 minutes. The carrots should be tender-to-soft—if they're still firm, put them back in for another minute. Drain.

4. Transfer the carrots to a blender or food processor and puree until very smooth. Scrape the carrots into a large bowl, add in the remaining ingredients, and whisk until well combined. Take care not to overbeat the mixture—if air bubbles form, let it sit for a few minutes before continuing on and allow the bubbles to deflate.

5. Pour the mixture into the prepared baking dish. Bake until the custard is set but still a bit wobbly in the middle, about 1 hour. It will firm up as it cools. Serve warm.

---

* If you don't want to open a big jar of applesauce just for this recipe, often the snack packs sold in the grocery store are each the 4-ounce size you'll need.

BOURSIN BAKED MASHED POTATOES

These tangy, herbed potatoes taste incredible right from the stovetop, a little time in the oven gives them an irresistible buttery crust (and pretty browned top) that's well worth waiting for. I find that a potato ricer makes the fluffiest mashed potatoes, and I highly recommend using one, but you can always make these potatoes with a regular masher as well.

 Makes 8 to 10 servings

INGREDIENTS:

3 pounds Yukon gold potatoes, peeled and quartered

1½ cups buttermilk

4 tablespoons unsalted butter, divided

1 (5.2 ounce) package Boursin cheese, or other spreadable garlic-herb cheese

1 teaspoon coarse salt

½ teaspoon freshly ground black pepper

Continued on next page

BOURSIN BAKED MASHED
POTATOES—*continued*

DIRECTIONS:

1. **Heat the oven to 425° F.**

2. Grease an 8x8-inch glass or ceramic baking dish or metal baking pan with butter or cooking spray.

3. Place the potatoes in a stockpot and add enough cold water to cover by an inch. Stir in a teaspoon of salt. Bring the water to a boil, then boil for another 20 minutes or until the potatoes are fork-tender. Drain.

4. Place the buttermilk and 3 tablespoons of butter in the same stockpot. When the potatoes are just cool enough to handle, press them through a potato ricer into the stockpot (or mash them in the stockpot with a potato masher). Mix in the cheese, salt, and pepper until incorporated.

5. Scrape the potatoes into the prepared baking dish—you can make decorative swirls with your spatula, if you like. Dot the top of the potatoes with the remaining tablespoon of butter.

6. Cover the dish with aluminum foil and bake for 15 minutes. Remove the foil and continue baking until the potatoes are lightly browned on top, 15 to 20 minutes.

CHEESY BROCCOLI CASSEROLE

I can't remember when my mom started making this casserole at our holiday gatherings, but it's been a family standby for years. Even the kids—make that *especially* the kids—love it, thanks to the hefty dose of cheese that accompanies the broccoli. It's one of those comfort food classics that pairs really well with just about any kind of roast, and will make you quite popular at a potluck.

 Makes 6 to 8 servings

INGREDIENTS:

3 broccoli crowns, cut into florets

2 tablespoons all-purpose flour

1 tablespoon unsalted butter

¼ cup diced yellow onion

1 large egg, beaten

8 ounces regular or reduced-fat cottage cheese

1 cup (about 4 ounces) shredded low-moisture mozzarella cheese

1 cup (about 4 ounces) shredded sharp cheddar cheese

½ teaspoon coarse salt

¼ teaspoon freshly ground black pepper

DIRECTIONS:

1. **Heat the oven to 325° F.** Grease an 8x8-inch glass or ceramic baking dish with butter or cooking spray. Alternatively, for a metal baking pan, heat the oven to 350° F and prepare the pan in the same manner.

2. Place the broccoli florets in a large, microwave-safe bowl and cover it with plastic wrap, leaving an opening for steam to escape. Cook the broccoli in the microwave on high for 3 to 5 minutes until it's tender. Drain, then toss the florets with the flour to absorb any excess water. Set aside.

3. Melt the butter in a small skillet over medium heat. Add the onions and cook, stirring occasionally, until the onions are translucent, about 10 minutes.

Continued on next page

4. Add the cooked onions to the broccoli mixture, as well as the egg, cottage cheese, all but about a handful of the mozzarella and cheddar cheeses, salt, and pepper. Mix until well combined. Transfer the mixture to the prepared dish or pan, spreading it to the edges in an even layer. Sprinkle the remaining cheese on top.

5. Bake the casserole until it's bubbly and lightly browned on top, 30 to 35 minutes.

CORN PUDDING

This sweet and savory side is another favorite from my mom's family gathering repertoire. Not only is it an incredibly simple dish to pull together, it's also one I can easily make ahead and reheat later. It also happens to be addictively delicious.

G C **Makes 8 to 10 servings**

INGREDIENTS:

3 large eggs
1 cup heavy cream
4 tablespoons unsalted butter, melted and cooled
2 tablespoons sugar
2 tablespoons all-purpose flour

1 teaspoon baking powder
¾ teaspoon coarse salt
3 cups fresh corn kernels or 1 (16-ounce) package frozen kernels, thawed

DIRECTIONS:

1. **Heat the oven to 350° F.**

2. Grease an 8x8-inch glass or ceramic baking dish with butter or cooking spray.

3. In a large bowl, whisk together the eggs, cream, and melted butter. Separately, in a small bowl, whisk together the sugar, flour, baking powder, and salt. Add the dry ingredients to the wet ingredients and whisk until smooth. Stir in the corn. Pour the mixture into the prepared pan.

4. Bake until golden brown on top and set in the middle, about 50 minutes.

LAYERED SPINACH, ARTICHOKE AND CRAB DIP

What goes faster at a potluck than a hot cheesy dip? Spinach dip, artichoke dip, crab dip—I love them all. I could never choose a favorite, and with this dip I don't have to. I could mix them all together, but by creating layers I can taste each flavor individually (while still getting one epic combined bite).

 **Makes 6 to 8 servings**

INGREDIENTS:

1 cup (about 4 ounces) grated Parmesan cheese

1 cup (about 4 ounces) grated Asiago cheese, divided

½ cup mayonnaise, regular or reduced-fat

½ cup sour cream, regular or reduced-fat

4 ounces cream cheese, at room temperature

1 tablespoon chopped fresh chives

1 tablespoon freshly squeezed lemon juice

½ teaspoon coarse salt

⅛ teaspoon freshly ground black pepper

8 ounces jumbo lump crabmeat

6 ounces artichoke hearts

1¼ cups (5 ounces) frozen chopped spinach, thawed

Corn tortilla chips, for serving

> **GIVE A GOOD SQUEEZE:** You'll want to get rid of as much moisture from the spinach and artichokes as you can so your dip doesn't turn watery. An easy way to do this is to put a handful of vegetables in a doubled-up paper towel and squeeze until no more water comes out.

Continued on next page

DIRECTIONS:

1. **Heat the oven to 400° F.**

2. In a large bowl, mix together the Parmesan, half the Asiago cheese, mayonnaise, sour cream, cream cheese, chives, lemon juice, salt, and pepper. Spread a third of the cheese mixture on the bottom of an 8x8-inch glass or ceramic baking dish. Scatter the crabmeat all over the cheese mixture. Spread half of the remaining cheese mixture on top of the crabmeat. Squeeze any excess liquid or oil from the artichoke hearts, roughly chop them, and arrange them in a layer on top of the cheese mixture. Squeeze any excess water from the spinach, stir it in with the remaining third of the cheese mixture, and spread it over the artichoke hearts. Sprinkle the remaining Asiago cheese on top.

3. Cover the dish with foil and bake for 20 minutes. Uncover and bake until it's bubbly and browned on top, another 25 to 30 minutes. Serve with tortilla chips.

On the Side

NATE'S COCONUT GRANOLA BARS

I created these crunchy granola bars especially for my 11-year old nephew, who is among the millions of people these days who need to pay close attention to the ingredients in dishes, due to food allergies and intolerances. These are slow-baked, lightly sweet, coconutty bars, that just happen to be gluten-, dairy-, and nut-free. It turns out I prefer them this way! I'll bet you will too.

 Makes 12 bars

INGREDIENTS:

1¾ cups old-fashioned rolled oats
½ cup sweetened shredded coconut
3 tablespoons melted coconut oil*
¼ cup honey

¼ cup brown rice syrup
2 teaspoons vanilla extract
⅛ teaspoon coarse salt
⅛ teaspoon freshly grated nutmeg

DIRECTIONS:

1. **Heat the oven to 300° F.**

2. **Line an 8x8-inch metal baking pan with parchment (see page 3 for a tutorial).**

I melt the coconut oil in a glass measuring cup in the microwave on high for about 30 seconds. After pouring out the oil, I use the same glass to measure the honey and brown rice syrup—the residual oil helps these otherwise sticky ingredients slide out of the glass easily.

Continued on next page

3. Grind ¼ cup of the oats in a food processor (it's an easy job for a mini-prep processor) or coffee grinder. Add the ground oats and all of the remaining ingredients to a large bowl. Mix well. Transfer the oat mixture to the prepared baking pan and pack it firmly with a spatula (go over it a few times to get it really good and packed—if it's sticking to your spatula, wrap your spatula with a piece of plastic wrap).

4. Bake until the bars are golden brown and aromatic, 45 to 50 minutes. Remove them from the oven and carefully pack the mixture down really well again with a spatula. Cool the bars in the pan for 15 minutes, then lift out the parchment and cut into bars while still warm. Allow the bars to cool completely on a cooling rack before serving. Extra bars will stay fresh in an airtight container for up to a week.

BREEZY BRUNCH

FLUFFY BAKED OMELET WITH PICO DE GALLO

I'm like a little kid when it comes to watching food rise in the oven. My eyes are practically glued to the oven window, observing the puffing and browning action. The whipped eggs in this baked omelet start out without much action, but before too long they lift higher and higher, nearly edging themselves out of the dish. This is some fascinating kitchen entertainment!

Continued on next page

Things settle down a bit once the omelet is out of the oven, but it still remains light and fluffy. Fresh pico de gallo makes a simple, flavorful topping—to dial down the heat, I omit the jalapeño when I prepare this for my children.

 **Makes 9 servings**

INGREDIENTS:

Omelet:

10 large eggs
1 cup whole milk
¾ teaspoon coarse salt
¼ teaspoon freshly ground
 black pepper
1 cup (about 4 ounces) shredded sharp
 cheddar or Jack cheese

Pico de Gallo:

2 cups seeded, diced tomatoes
 (about 3 medium)
¼ cup finely chopped red onion
 (about ¼ medium)
¼ cup chopped fresh cilantro
1 tablespoon seeded and finely
 chopped jalapeño pepper (about 1)
 (optional)
1 tablespoon freshly squeezed lime
 juice (about ½ lime)
⅛ teaspoon coarse salt

DIRECTIONS:

1. **Heat the oven to 450° F.**

2. Set a rack in the upper third of the oven. Grease an 8x8-inch glass or ceramic baking dish with butter or cooking spray.

3. In a large bowl, whisk together the eggs, milk, salt, and pepper. Mix in the cheese. Pour the mixture into the prepared dish. Bake until the omelet is set in the middle, puffed (it will puff quite a bit, but will settle down as it cools) and lightly browned on top, about 20 minutes.

4. While the omelet is baking, add all of the pico de gallo ingredients to a medium bowl and stir to combine. Allow the omelet to cool for several minutes, then, with a slotted spoon, top it with pico de gallo before serving.

ROASTED HASH BROWNS WITH BACON AND SCALLIONS

There's a certain wow factor when you bring a pan of homemade hash browns to a brunch table, especially when bits of bacon and scallions are peeking out from between the potato strands. It makes an impressive special occasion dish, yet it's rather simple to prepare. After many, many batches of these hash browns, I've found that Yukon Golds work best for a soft interior and a crispy, golden exterior.

G C M **Makes 6 to 8 servings**

INGREDIENTS:

6 strips bacon, cut into ½-inch pieces

1½ pounds Yukon Gold potatoes, scrubbed and peeled

4 scallions, divided

½ teaspoon coarse salt

¼ teaspoon freshly ground black pepper

4 tablespoons unsalted butter, divided

DIRECTIONS:

1. **Heat the oven to 375° F.**

2. Line an 8x8-inch glass or ceramic baking dish or metal baking pan with parchment (see the tutorial on page 3).

3. Place the bacon pieces in a large skillet and set over medium heat. Cook the bacon, stirring occasionally, until it's browned and crisp. With a slotted spoon, transfer the cooked bacon to a paper towel-lined plate.

4. Fill a large bowl with cold water. Shred the potatoes directly into the water to keep them from discoloring (keep the peeled whole potatoes in the water until you're ready to shred them). In two or three batches, transfer handfuls of the shredded potatoes to a clean towel, roll it up, twist the ends and wring out as much water as possible—this will enable them to crisp up in the oven. Keep twisting and wringing until it's good and squeezed. Transfer the towel-dried potatoes to a large bowl.

Continued on next page

ROASTED HASH BROWNS WITH BACON AND SCALLIONS—*continued*

5. Chop three of the scallions and add them to the bowl with the potatoes, along with the cooked bacon, salt, and pepper. Melt 3 tablespoons of the butter in a microwave-safe bowl in the microwave on high for 1 minute (or in a small saucepan over medium heat) and pour evenly over the potatoes. Stir until the mixture is well combined. Spoon the potatoes into the prepared dish or pan and spread them in an even layer, taking care not to pack them down. Break up the remaining tablespoon of butter into small pieces and dot all over the top.

6. Bake until the potatoes are cooked through, crispy, and golden brown on top, about 1 hour 15 minutes. Chop the remaining scallion, and scatter it over the top as garnish.

[GET A HEAD START: If you don't have time in the morning for these hash browns to slowly roast in the oven, you can always bake them the night before and reheat them before serving.]

BACON, SPINACH AND GRUYÈRE CRUSTLESS QUICHE

When I was about 10 years old, I proclaimed quiche my favorite food—mostly because I loved the notion of a savory pie you could eat for breakfast, lunch, or dinner—but also because I was simply fascinated with a word that was spelled "quiche" but pronounced "keesh." My mom loved it because she could put spinach in our "keesh" and my sisters and I would excitedly eat it.

The "quick crust" in this recipe, made with bread crumbs and a layer of cheese, does a great job of holding the pie together when I don't have the time (or the inclination) to roll out a traditional crust.

 **Makes 6 to 8 servings**

INGREDIENTS:

2 tablespoons dry bread crumbs
6 slices bacon, chopped into
   ½-inch strips
1 cup chopped sweet onions
   (e.g., Vidalia, Walla Walla, or Maui)
1 cup frozen chopped spinach, thawed
1 tablespoon all-purpose flour
1½ cups (about 6 ounces) shredded
   Gruyère cheese

4 large eggs
1 cup heavy cream
1 cup whole milk
½ teaspoon coarse salt
⅛ teaspoon freshly ground
   black pepper
Pinch ground nutmeg

DIRECTIONS:

1. **Heat the oven to 350° F.**

2. Grease an 8x8-inch glass or ceramic baking dish with butter. Sprinkle the bottom and sides of the dish with bread crumbs. Alternatively, for a metal baking pan, heat the oven to 375°F and prepare the pan in the same manner.

Continued on next page

BACON, SPINACH AND GRUYÈRE
CRUSTLESS QUICHE—*continued*

3. Cook the bacon strips in a large skillet over medium heat until they're browned and crisped. With a slotted spoon, transfer the cooked bacon to a paper towel-lined plate. Pour off all but 1 tablespoon of the rendered bacon fat and return the pan to the heat. Add the onions and cook, stirring occasionally, until they're softened, 8 to 10 minutes. Set aside. Wring the thawed spinach inside a clean towel to remove as much moisture as possible. Add the spinach, bacon, and flour to the pan with the onions and stir to combine (the flour will help to absorb excess liquid).

4. Scatter half of the cheese evenly over the bottom of the prepared dish or pan. Top it with the spinach mixture in an even layer, followed by the remaining cheese.

5. In a large bowl, whisk together the eggs, cream, milk, salt, pepper, and nutmeg. Pour the mixture over the cheese.

6. Bake until the custard is set in the middle and the top is golden, 40 to 50 minutes. Allow the quiche to cool until it's warm or at room temperature before cutting and serving.

BAKED BLUEBERRY OATMEAL

My kids especially love to help me make dishes like these—there's lots for them to measure and mix, no knives needed (unless you chop the nuts yourself), and no time at the stove. They go play for 40 minutes while it's in the oven and, *voilà*, they've baked a moist, delicious "oatmeal cake." We like to freeze individual portions to pull out for quick hot breakfasts during the week.

G C M **Yield: 9 servings**

INGREDIENTS:

3 cups rolled oats

1½ cups whole milk

½ cup dark brown sugar

⅓ cup dried blueberries*

¼ cup chopped pecans

4 tablespoons unsalted butter, melted

2 tablespoons maple syrup

2 teaspoons baking powder

1 teaspoon vanilla extract

1½ teaspoons ground cinnamon

½ teaspoon coarse salt

2 large eggs, lightly beaten

* Look for dried blueberries alongside raisins and other dried fruit at the store.

DIRECTIONS:

1. **Heat the oven to 325° F.**

2. Grease an 8x8-inch glass or ceramic baking dish with butter or cooking spray. Alternatively, for a metal baking pan, heat the oven to 350° F and prepare the pan in a similar manner.

3. Mix all of the ingredients together in a large bowl until they're well combined.

4. Pour the mixture into the prepared baking dish or pan. Bake until fully set and golden brown on top, about 40 minutes.

[BREAKFAST FOR DESSERT? The recipe testers unanimously decided they would love to enjoy this dish with a nice scoop of vanilla ice cream. You be the judge!]

ORANGE CUSTARD FRENCH TOAST

MAKE IT AHEAD: If you're not an early riser (I'm right there with you!) you can also refrigerate this dish overnight, unbaked, and bake it the next morning.

As if the sweeping views of the Pacific weren't enough, Brockton Villa restaurant in La Jolla, California also entices crowds of customers with their "Coast Toast"—a citrusy, soufflé-like version of French toast. It was our standard brunch recommendation for out-of-towners when we lived in San Diego; you simply can't beat it. With a nod to "Coast Toast," my Orange Custard French Toast is aromatic, fluffy, and baked casserole-style for a very special brunch at home.

G C **Makes 4 to 8 servings**

INGREDIENTS:

½ pound challah bread, sliced about ¾-inch thick

1½ cups heavy cream

4 large eggs

½ cup freshly squeezed orange juice (from 1 to 2 large oranges)

¼ cup sugar

1 tablespoon vanilla extract

2 teaspoons orange zest

¼ cup sliced almonds

Confectioners' sugar, for dusting

DIRECTIONS:

1. **Heat the oven to 325° F.**

2. Spray an 8x8-inch ceramic or glass baking dish with cooking spray.

Continued on next page

3. Arrange the bread slices in tiled rows in the prepared dish (you might need to cut a few in half to make them fit). In a large bowl, whisk together the cream, eggs, juice, sugar, vanilla, and zest. Pour the mixture over the bread slices, making sure each slice is saturated. Cover the dish with foil and refrigerate for at least an hour.

4. Bake, covered, for 30 minutes. Remove the foil, sprinkle on the almonds, and continue baking until the casserole is puffed and golden, 30 to 35 minutes. Dust with confectioners' sugar before serving.

CARAMELIZED BANANA PANCAKE SQUARES

I was captivated by the idea of caramelizing bananas in the bottom of a baking dish and then pouring in my favorite buttermilk pancake batter on top to make upside-down cake-style pancake squares. And it worked gloriously! You might even say these pancakes are "self-saucing," with the sweet banana and caramel layer soaking into the squares like syrup. Upside-down cake for breakfast!

 **Makes 9 servings**

INGREDIENTS:

- 1 tablespoon unsalted butter, plus more for greasing the dish
- 2 ripe bananas, thinly sliced
- 2 tablespoons firmly packed brown sugar
- 1¼ cups all-purpose flour
- 1 tablespoon sugar

- 1 teaspoon baking powder
- ½ teaspoon baking soda
- ¼ teaspoon coarse salt
- 1 cup buttermilk
- 1 large egg
- 2 tablespoons vegetable oil
- 2 teaspoons vanilla extract

Continued on next page

DIRECTIONS:

1. **Heat the oven to 350° F.**

2. Grease an 8x8-inch glass or ceramic baking dish with butter.

3. Melt the tablespoon of butter in the dish while the oven heats. Swirl the pan to coat the bottom with butter. Arrange banana slices, as many as will neatly fit, in an even layer on the bottom of the dish, and sprinkle brown sugar on top. Once the oven is heated, bake the bananas until the brown sugar is melted and bubbly—the bananas and caramel will become fragrant.

4. While the bananas are caramelizing, whisk together the flour, sugar, baking powder, baking soda, and salt in a large bowl. Separately, whisk the buttermilk, egg, oil, and vanilla in a medium bowl or measuring cup. Add the wet ingredients to the dry ingredients and mix until just combined. Pour the pancake batter over the caramelized bananas, spreading it in an even layer with a spatula.

5. Bake until the pancake is puffed and lightly golden, and a toothpick inserted in the center comes out clean, about 25 minutes. Cut into squares and lift them carefully from the pan with a spatula. Serve banana-side up!

OVERNIGHT APPLE CINNAMON ROLLS WITH CIDER GLAZE

I've tried, and I honestly cannot imagine any better aroma in the world to wake up to than that of cinnamon rolls baking in the oven. I have actually observed my paja-ma-clad children dreamily follow their noses to the kitchen to discover the source of the deliciousness. Adding fresh sweet apples and cider to the mix gives the rolls an even more enticing twist.

It does, of course, take some time to prepare these rolls, but that only makes them an extra special treat. Getting a head start the night before means a much shorter wait in the morning. Waiting is, by far, the most challenging step in this recipe!

G C **Makes 9 rolls**

INGREDIENTS:

Dough:

2 cups all-purpose
   flour, divided
1⅛ teaspoons instant
   (rapid-rise) yeast
½ teaspoon salt
½ cup whole milk
2 tablespoons apple cider
2 tablespoons unsalted
   butter
2 tablespoons sugar
1 large egg, beaten

Filling:

2 tablespoons unsalted
   butter, melted
3 tablespoons firmly
   packed brown sugar
2 tablespoons sugar
1 teaspoon ground
   cinnamon
¾ cup finely chopped
   apple (about 1 medium)
¼ cup chopped walnuts

Glaze:

¼ cup apple cider
¼ teaspoon cinnamon
Pinch salt
1 tablespoon unsalted
   butter
¼ cup confectioners sugar

Continued on next page

*Yes, you need to use a thermometer for this—if the liquids are too hot they may kill the yeast.

DIRECTIONS:

1. Line an 8x8-inch glass or ceramic baking dish or metal baking pan with parchment (see the tutorial on page 3).

2. In a small bowl, whisk together 1 cup of the flour, yeast, and salt. Set aside.

3. In a large microwave-safe bowl, heat the milk, cider, and butter on high for 60 to 90 seconds, until the butter is melted. Allow the mixture to cool to 120°F.* Mix in the sugar and egg. Mix in the flour mixture, then add enough of the remaining flour so it's easy to handle (e.g., not too sticky). Depending on the humidity in the room, you may or may not need all of the remaining flour.

4. Transfer the dough to a lightly floured surface and knead it for about 5 minutes. A good way to tell if you're done kneading is to poke your finger into the dough—if the indentation pops right back out it's ready. Let the dough rest for 10 minutes.

5. On a lightly floured surface, roll out the dough into a 9x9-inch square. Brush the butter for the filling all over the surface of the dough. In a small bowl, combine the sugars and cinnamon; sprinkle them over the butter. Scatter the apples and walnuts on top. Carefully and tightly roll up the dough. Slice the dough into 9 equal pieces (about 1-inch wide each), and arrange them, cut side down, in the prepared dish or pan. Leave space between each roll—they will rise and expand. Cover the dish or pan with plastic wrap and set in the refrigerator overnight, or for at least 8 hours.

Continued on next page

6. Uncover the dish or pan and set it out at room temperature an hour before you're ready to bake the rolls.

7. **Heat the oven to 350° F** for glass or ceramic dishes or 375° F for metal pans.

8. Bake until the rolls are lightly browned and a thermometer inserted in the center reads 190° F, about 25 minutes. If the rolls begin browning too fast, you can cover them lightly with foil.

9. To make the glaze, bring the cider, cinnamon, and salt to a boil in a small saucepan over medium heat. Lower the heat and simmer until the cider is reduced to 2 tablespoons, 4 to 5 minutes. Remove the saucepan from the heat and stir in the butter and confectioners sugar. Drizzle the glaze over the rolls right before serving.

BUTTERMILK BANANA CRUMB CAKE

PRECISION COUNTS: Take the time to measure the bananas to have the texture come out just right.

This is a mashup of two of my favorite breakfast baked goods—banana bread and crumb cake. It's bound to become an instant classic at your house, as it has at ours. The incredibly moist buttermilk banana bread part is based on a recipe I've loved for years from the *Mel's Kitchen Cafe* blog. Adding a New York-style crumb on top complements it spectacularly!

G C M **Makes 16 servings**

INGREDIENTS:

Topping:

½ cup firmly packed brown sugar

¼ cup sugar

2 teaspoons ground cinnamon

¼ teaspoon coarse salt

½ cup (1 stick) unsalted butter, melted

1¼ cups all-purpose flour

Cake:

1¾ cups all-purpose flour

1 teaspoon baking powder

¼ teaspoon salt

⅛ teaspoon baking soda

½ cup (1 stick) unsalted butter, softened

1 cup sugar

2 large eggs

1 cup mashed bananas (2 to 3 medium)

¼ cup buttermilk

2 teaspoons vanilla extract

Continued on next page

BUTTERMILK BANANA CRUMB
CAKE—*continued*

DIRECTIONS:

1. **Heat the oven to 325° F.**

2. Line an 8x8-inch glass or ceramic baking dish with parchment (see page 3 for a tutorial). Alternatively, for a metal pan, heat the oven to 350° F and prepare the pan in a similar manner.

3. To make the topping, whisk together the brown sugar, sugar, cinnamon, and salt in a medium bowl. Stir in the melted butter. Add the flour and combine the mixture with a fork until moist clumps form. Set the topping aside.

4. For the cake, whisk together the flour, baking powder, salt, and baking soda in a medium bowl.

5. In a large bowl, cream the butter and sugar together. Add the eggs, bananas, buttermilk, and vanilla and mix until well combined. Mix in the dry ingredients. Pour the batter into the prepared pan. Scatter the topping, in clumps, all over the top—there will be a lot of topping, it's key to this cake!

6. Bake until a toothpick inserted near the center comes out clean, 55 to 60 minutes. Cool completely before cutting into squares.

SWEET TREATS

TRIPLE CHOCOLATE SAUCEPAN BROWNIES

Did you know that the chocolate in brownies brings more than just rich flavor? It also determines the texture. Brownies made with cocoa powder will be chewier, while those made with melted chocolate will be fudgier. With this recipe, I use both ingredients for just the right balance of chewy and fudgy, plus chocolate chips to scatter little nuggets of chocolate throughout.

G C M **Makes 16 brownies**

INGREDIENTS:

½ cup (1 stick) unsalted butter
1 cup sugar
2 ounces bittersweet chocolate, roughly chopped
½ cup unsweetened cocoa powder
½ teaspoon coarse salt

½ teaspoon baking powder
2 teaspoons vanilla extract
2 large eggs
¾ cup all-purpose flour
1 cup semisweet chocolate chips
½ cup chopped pecans or walnuts

DIRECTIONS:

1. **Heat the oven to 325° F.**

2. Line an 8x8-inch glass or baking dish with parchment (see page 3 for a tutorial). Alternatively, for a metal baking pan, heat the oven to 350° F and prepare the pan in the same manner.

3. In a medium saucepan, melt the butter over medium-low heat. Add the sugar and stir until well combined and shiny. Remove the pan from the heat.

Continued on next page

TRIPLE CHOCOLATE SAUCEPAN
BROWNIES—*continued*

4. In a small microwave-safe bowl, heat the chocolate in the microwave at 50% power in 30 second increments, stirring after each heating, until it's fully melted (alternatively, you can melt the chocolate in a double-boiler on the stove). Pour the melted chocolate into the sugar mixture. Stir in the cocoa powder, salt, baking powder, and vanilla. Beat in each egg, one at a time. Mix in the flour, chocolate chips, and nuts until combined, reserving a small handful of chips and nuts to sprinkle on top before baking.

5. Spread the batter into the prepared dish or pan, and scatter the reserved chocolate chips and nuts over the top. Bake until the brownies are set in the middle, 25 to 28 minutes*. Cool completely before cutting.

---

* Unlike with cakes, you're not looking for the brownies to cook through completely in the middle—that will mean a dry brownie. Instead, you want it to be just set. Err on the side of gooey!

PUMPKIN CHEESECAKE SWIRL BLONDIES

There comes a time of year when people go a little crazy for pumpkin. Snapshots captioned with "first pumpkin spice latte of the season!" pop up in my Instagram feed and Pinterest practically turns solid orange. Bringing these spiced pumpkin blondies, with their marbled cheesecake tops, to an office potluck, team party, or bake sale is practically a guaranteed crowd pleaser. You may want to bake yourself an extra batch—because this tray is going home empty.

G C M **Makes 16 servings**

INGREDIENTS:

Cheesecake Topping:

8 ounces cream cheese, softened
¼ cup sugar
1 large egg
1 teaspoon vanilla extract

Pumpkin Blondies:

8 tablespoons (1 stick) unsalted butter
1 cup brown sugar
¼ cup pumpkin puree
1 large egg
2 teaspoons vanilla extract
1 cup all-purpose flour
½ teaspoon ground cinnamon
¼ teaspoon ground ginger
¼ teaspoon ground nutmeg
¼ teaspoon coarse salt

DIRECTIONS:

1. **Heat the oven to 325° F.**

2. Line an 8x8-inch glass or ceramic baking dish with parchment (see page 3 for a tutorial). Alternatively, for a metal baking pan, heat the oven to 350° F and prepare the pan in the same manner.

3. To prepare the topping, with an electric mixer or by hand with a wooden spoon, beat together the cream cheese, sugar, egg, and vanilla in a medium bowl until smooth. Set aside.

Continued on next page

PUMPKIN CHEESECAKE SWIRL
BLONDIES—*continued*

4. To prepare the blondies, melt the butter in a medium saucepan over medium heat. Remove the pan from the heat and beat in the brown sugar until smooth. Add the pumpkin, egg, and vanilla and beat until smooth.

5. In a small bowl, whisk together the flour, cinnamon, ginger, nutmeg, and salt. Add the flour mixture to the wet ingredients and mix until combined.

6. Pour all but about ½ cup of the blondie batter into the prepared dish or pan, spreading it in an even layer. Spoon on the cheesecake topping and spread it in an even layer. Spoon on the remaining blondie batter and draw a butter knife through the layers to create interesting swirls.

7. Bake until the blondies are set in the middle and a toothpick inserted near the center comes out clean, about 40 minutes. Allow the blondies to cool completely before lifting them out by the parchment and cutting into squares.

CHOCOLATE CHIP COOKIE BARS

I've told the story over and over again about the time my sister and I, when she was 9 and I was 11, attempted to bake six enormous chocolate chip cookies in our home ec class rather than the twenty-four regular-sized ones the recipe called for. We wound up with a mess (and a stern reprimand from the teacher—yikes!). Thankfully, that mishap didn't deter me from experimenting with cookie dough. On the contrary... I'll bake chocolate chip cookies in any way I can dream up!

 Makes 16 bars

INGREDIENTS:

½ cup (1 stick) unsalted
   butter, softened
¾ cup firmly packed dark brown sugar
¼ cup sugar
1 large egg
2 teaspoons vanilla extract

1¾ cups all-purpose flour
½ teaspoon baking soda
½ teaspoon salt
1¼ cups semisweet chocolate
   chips, divided

DIRECTIONS:

1. **Heat the oven to 350° F.**

2. Line an 8x8-inch metal baking pan with parchment paper (see page 3 for a tutorial).

3. Beat the butter and both sugars together for several minutes until they're light and fluffy, either with an electric mixer or by hand with a wooden spoon in a large bowl. Beat in the egg and vanilla until they're well combined. Separately, whisk together the flour, baking soda, and salt in a medium bowl. Add the dry ingredients to the wet ingredients and mix until they're well combined. Fold in 1 cup of the chocolate chips.

Continued on next page

CHOCOLATE CHIP COOKIE
BARS—*continued*

BETTER YET:
Cutting a pan of chocolate chip cookies into bars takes a whole lot less effort than scooping individual drop cookies!

4. Pour the dough into the prepared pan, spreading it to the edges and corners (it doesn't have to be perfect—the dough will further spread in the oven). Bake until the bars are fully set and lightly browned on top, about 25 minutes. Allow them to cool completely in the pan on a cooling rack.

5. In a small microwave-safe bowl, heat the remaining chocolate chips in the microwave at 50% power in 30 second increments, stirring after each heating, until they're fully melted (alternatively, you can melt the chocolate in a double-boiler on the stove). Drizzle the melted chocolate over the cooled cookie bars before cutting and serving.

TOP 8 BAKE SALE TREATS

These sweet 8x8 treats are perfect candidates for a good old-fashioned bake sale—they're convenient to portion and wrap individually, and they display beautifully as well. Bring one of these items and expect to be asked to bake for all future events!

1. Triple Chocolate Saucepan Brownies* (page 127)

2. Pumpkin Cheesecake Swirl Blondies (page 129)

3. Chocolate Chip Cookie Bars (page 132)

4. Dreamy Caramel Bars* (page 137)

5. Buttermilk Banana Crumb Cake (page 123)

6. Apple-Almond Cake* (page 144)

7. Mary's Best Baklava* (page 160)

8. Vanilla Chai Fudge (page 165)

* Since these recipes contain nuts, out of concern for bake sale customers who may be allergic, you may want to either omit the nuts altogether or (especially in the case of the Apple-Almond Cake and Mary's Best Baklava where nuts are a key ingredient) clearly label them as containing nuts.

DREAMY CARAMEL BARS

I hadn't heard of carmelita bars until one weekend when I came across them at two different bakeries (yes, it's quite normal for me to visit multiple bakeries in a weekend!). I was instantly smitten by these crumbly cookie bars, layered with caramel and chocolate, and I was determined to bake my own at home.

I call my version Dreamy Caramel Bars to pay homage to the real, homemade caramel inside. Most recipes call for melting caramel candies to make the caramel layer, but to me, there are few better things in this world than caramel made from scratch. The rich burnt sugar flavor is beyond compare!

 Makes 9 servings

INGREDIENTS:

Caramel:

½ cup sugar
3 tablespoons cold
   unsalted butter, diced
2 tablespoons heavy
   cream
1 teaspoon vanilla extract
Pinch coarse salt

Crust:

8 tablespoons unsalted
   butter, melted
¾ cup brown sugar
2 teaspoons vanilla
   extract
1 cup all-purpose flour
1 cup rolled oats
½ teaspoon baking soda
½ teaspoon coarse salt

Filling:

¼ cup chopped pecans
3 ounces semisweet
   chocolate, chopped

DIRECTIONS:

1. **Heat the oven to 350° F.**

2. Line an 8x8-inch metal baking pan with parchment (see page 3 for a tutorial).

Continued on next page

3. To make the caramel, heat the sugar in a medium-sized (2-quart), heavy-bottomed sauce pan over medium heat. Start whisking once the sugar begins to melt. It will initially clump into tiny balls but will eventually melt evenly. When it begins to boil, stop whisking—you don't want the super-hot sugar to splash out onto you. The sugar will start to turn an amber color—swirl the pan occasionally to keep it from burning. Once all the sugar is melted, slide in the butter and whisk until melted. Remove the pan from the heat and whisk in the cream, vanilla, and salt—the caramel will bubble up a bit! Set the pan aside.

4. To make the crust, stir the butter and brown sugar together in a medium bowl with a wooden spoon until they're fully combined—this may take a minute or two. Stir in the vanilla. Add the flour, oats, baking soda, and salt and stir until the dough is combined.

5. Transfer half of the dough to the prepared baking pan, pressing it with your fingers to create an even layer on the bottom of the pan, all the way to the edges. Bake the crust for 12 minutes—it should be cooked through and golden. Remove the pan from the oven, but keep the oven on.

6. With a rubber spatula, scrape the caramel into the baking pan and spread evenly over the warm crust. Scatter the pecans and chocolate over the caramel. Drop pinches of the remaining crust dough all over the top.

7. Bake until the crust is golden, 15 to 18 minutes. Allow the bars to cool completely before cutting them.

CHOCOLATE CRAVING CAKE

Chocolate cravings are real, and cannot go ignored! When one strikes, turn to a little square cake like this to save the day. One layer, no frills—just the moistest chocolate cake ever, blanketed in an easy chocolate sour cream ganache. Craving satisfied.

G C M **Makes 9 servings**

INGREDIENTS:

Cake:

1 cup all-purpose flour
1 cup sugar
½ cup unsweetened cocoa powder
¾ teaspoon baking powder
¾ teaspoon baking soda
½ teaspoon coarse salt
1 large egg
½ cup whole milk
¼ cup vegetable oil
2 teaspoons vanilla extract
½ cup boiling water

Frosting:

1 cup semisweet chocolate chips
½ cup sour cream, regular or
   reduced-fat
1 teaspoon vanilla extract

DIRECTIONS:

1. **Heat the oven to 300° F.**

2. Line an 8x8-inch glass or ceramic baking dish with parchment (see page 3 for a tutorial) and grease the parchment with butter or spray it with baking spray. Alternatively, for a metal baking pan, heat the oven to 325°F and prepare the pan in the same manner.

Continued on next page

3. Mix the flour, sugar, cocoa powder, baking powder, baking soda, and salt in a large bowl or mixer bowl. Add the egg, milk, oil, and vanilla to the dry ingredients (no need to combine them in a separate bowl) and beat by hand with a wooden spoon, or with an electric mixer on medium speed, for 2 minutes. Stir in the boiling water—the batter will be very thin, like hot cocoa, at this point.

4. Pour the batter into the prepared dish or pan. Bake until a toothpick inserted in the center comes out clean, 35 to 40 minutes. Cool on a rack for 10 minutes, then lift out the cake by the parchment, and continue cooling to room temperature.

5. While the cake cools, make the frosting. In a medium microwave-safe bowl, heat the chocolate chips in the microwave at 50% power in 30 second increments, stirring after each heating, until they're fully melted (or melt chocolate on the stovetop in a double boiler). Add the sour cream and vanilla and beat by hand with a wooden spoon or with an electric mixer on medium speed until the frosting is well combined and fluffy.

6. Transfer the cooled cake to a serving plate and frost the top and sides. Serve at room temperature. Refrigerate any leftovers.

CINNAMON TRES LECHES CAKE

The first tres leches cake I ever made—right before a party—was a complete flop. The sponge cake came out heavy and dry and it hardly soaked up any of the milks at all. I served a carton of ice cream for dessert that night and steered clear of baking tres leches cakes for a long time. Fast forward a few years, I signed up to bring a Mexican dessert to a Cinco de Mayo potluck. The time had come to revisit tres leches.

With the new recipe, everything went as it should—the sponge cake was light and puffy, the milks soaked right in, and the cinnamon flavor I chose reminded me of a fresh churro. It was incredible! Despite the lengthy directions, it's actually a rather simple cake—one you're going to want to make again and again.

 Makes 16 servings

INGREDIENTS:

Cake:
4 large eggs, separated
½ cup sugar
1 cup all-purpose flour
1 teaspoon ground
cinnamon

Milks:
¾ cup whole milk
½ cup plus 2 tablespoons
sweetened condensed
milk
½ cup evaporated milk
2 teaspoons vanilla
extract

Topping:
1 cup heavy whipping
cream
2 tablespoons
confectioners' sugar
1 teaspoon vanilla extract
Ground cinnamon, for
sprinkling

Continued on next page

CINNAMON TRES LECHES CAKE—*continued*

*I find it easiest to beat the egg yolks and whites using an electric hand mixer, but you can always use a stand mixer instead—you'll just need to transfer the beaten yolks to a clean bowl, then wash both the beater and the mixer bowl before beating the whites.

DIRECTIONS:

1. **Heat the oven to 375° F.**

2. Grease an 8x8-inch glass or ceramic baking dish with butter or baking spray.

3. Place the egg yolks in a small mixing bowl* and beat them with a hand mixer for 5 minutes—they will turn from a bright orange-yellow color to pale yellow as air is beaten into them. Set the yolks aside, and wash the beaters. Place the egg whites in a large mixing bowl and beat them with the hand mixer until soft peaks form, 2 to 3 minutes. While still beating, gradually add in the sugar and continue beating until the mixture is thick and opaque, and holds stiff peaks.

4. Drizzle the egg yolks over the egg whites and gently fold them into the whites, without deflating them too much, until they're incorporated. Sprinkle the flour and cinnamon over the top of the egg mixture and gently fold them in, without over mixing, until there are no more flour streaks.

5. Scrape the batter to the prepared pan, gently smoothing the batter to the corners of the dish. Bake until a toothpick inserted at the center comes out clean and the top is lightly browned, 20 to 25 minutes.

6. While the cake is baking, stir together the milk, sweetened condensed milk, evaporated milk, and vanilla in a medium bowl.

Continued on next page

7. Transfer the cake to a cooling rack. Poke holes all over the cake with a toothpick or skewer. Allow the cake the cool completely. Pour the milk mixture all over the cooled cake. If you're ready to serve immediately, you can proceed to the next step. Or you can chill the cake for several hours or overnight at this point.

8. Place the cream, confectioners' sugar, and vanilla in a medium mixing bowl and whip with the hand mixer until soft peaks form. Spread an even layer of whipped cream over the cake and sprinkle a little cinnamon on top.

ONE MORE THING: To make a tres leches cake in this smaller 8x8 size you won't need the entire cans of sweetened condensed or evaporated milks. You can always double the recipe to make two cakes, or one 13x9-inch cake.

APPLE-ALMOND CAKE

When my sister Julie was in preschool she wrote a "recipe" for an apple cake. In my 7-year old maturity, I remember laughing and laughing... whoever heard of an apple cake?! Cakes were either chocolate or vanilla, right? Kids!

Apple cake, I thankfully learned, is real and, especially during autumn apple-picking season, one of my favorites. I love to serve this almond version still a bit warm, with a scoop of vanilla ice cream on top.

G C M **Makes 9 servings**

INGREDIENTS:

Cake:

1 cup all-purpose flour
½ cup almond flour*
2 teaspoons baking powder
½ teaspoon salt
½ teaspoon ground cinnamon
¼ teaspoon ground nutmeg
½ cup (1 stick) unsalted butter, softened
½ cup sugar
⅓ cup firmly packed brown sugar
2 large eggs
1 teaspoon almond extract
1 cup grated apple (about 1 large, peeled and cored)

Topping:

1 large apple, peeled, cored, and thinly sliced
1 tablespoon sugar
Confectioners sugar, for dusting

*You can usually find almond flour in the same aisle as all-purpose flour in the grocery store. I buy it at Costco and store it in the freezer.

Continued on next page

DIRECTIONS:

1. **Heat the oven to 325° F.**

2. Line an 8x8-inch glass or ceramic baking dish with parchment (see page 3 for a tutorial). Alternatively, for a metal baking pan, heat the oven to 350° F and prepare the pan in a similar manner.

3. In a small bowl, whisk together the flour, almond flour, baking powder, salt, cinnamon, and nutmeg. Set aside.

4. In a large bowl, beat the butter and both sugars together with an electric mixer or by hand with a wooden spoon, until light and fluffy. Add the eggs and almond extract and mix until combined. Stir in the grated apple. Add the flour mixture and mix until just combined. Scrape the batter into the prepared pan with a rubber spatula, spreading it to the edges and corners.

5. Arrange the sliced apples in a tiled pattern on top of the batter. Sprinkle the granulated sugar over the apples.

6. Bake until a toothpick inserted at the center of the cake comes out clean, 45 to 50 minutes. Allow the cake to cool before dusting the top with confectioners sugar and serving.

BALSAMIC CHERRIES WITH GRAHAM CRACKER CRUMBLE

Sunnyvale, California may be best known today for being the home of Yahoo! and countless other Silicon Valley giants, but when I was growing up there, cherry orchards held the greater claim to fame. Every spring I would look forward to stopping by the C.J. Olson cherry stand for the sweetest locally grown Bing cherries. I always just ate them straight from the pint container, but these days I don't mind them at all roasted with good balsamic vinegar beneath a crunchy streusel topping and a dollop of vanilla Greek yogurt on top, for a cool, creamy finish.

G C **Makes 6 to 8 servings**

INGREDIENTS:

Filling:

2 pounds fresh sweet cherries, pitted

⅓ cup sugar

1 tablespoon balsamic vinegar

2 tablespoon cornstarch

Topping:

½ cup firmly packed brown sugar

½ cup all-purpose flour

½ cup graham cracker crumbs

2 tablespoons sugar

1 teaspoon ground cinnamon

¼ teaspoon coarse salt

6 tablespoons unsalted butter, melted

Continued on next page

DIRECTIONS:

1. **Heat the oven to 375° F.**

2. Mix the cherries, sugar, balsamic vinegar, and cornstarch in an 8x8-inch glass or ceramic baking dish.

3. In a medium bowl, mix the brown sugar, flour, graham cracker crumbs, sugar, cinnamon, and salt. Pour the melted butter over the mixture and stir until a crumbly paste forms. Drop the topping in clumps all over the cherries in the baking dish (you might opt not to use all of the topping, but I doubt you'll regret it if you go for it!).

4. Bake until the cherries are bubbly and the topping is browned, 40 to 45 minutes.

BLUEBERRY COBBLER WITH CORNMEAL CREAM BISCUITS

When summer brings loads of fresh blueberries to the farmers market (or your own bushes, if you're so lucky) here is one cobbler recipe that will most definitely do them justice. I eat this with a spoon—it slides through the cold scoop of ice cream on top, getting a little melted as it hits the warm, sugar-topped cornmeal biscuit until finally descending into the juicy blueberry grotto at the bottom. It's more than a cobbler—it's an experience!

G C **Makes 9 servings**

INGREDIENTS:

6 cups (3 pints) fresh blueberries, rinsed and drained

½ cup plus 2 tablespoons sugar, divided

3 tablespoons cornstarch

1 tablespoon finely grated lemon zest

1 tablespoon freshly squeezed lemon juice

1½ cups all-purpose flour

⅓ cup cornmeal

2 teaspoons baking powder

½ teaspoon coarse salt

½ cup (1 stick) cold unsalted butter, cut into thin pats

¾ cup cold heavy cream, plus more for brushing

2 teaspoons raw turbinado sugar

Vanilla ice cream, for serving (optional)

DIRECTIONS:

1. **Heat the oven to 375° F.**

2. Place the blueberries in a large bowl. Add ½ cup of sugar, cornstarch, lemon zest, and lemon juice and gently stir to combine. Transfer the blueberry mixture to an 8x8-inch glass or ceramic baking dish.

Continued on next page

3. In another large bowl, whisk together the flour, cornmeal, the remaining 2 tablespoons of sugar, baking powder, and salt. Add the butter and, with a pastry blender or your fingers, work it in until the mixture resembles coarse crumbs. Stir in the cream just until combined.

4. Drop 9 small handfuls of dough on top of the blueberries, leaving space between each biscuit (if you have any dough left over, go ahead and bake yourself a little bonus biscuit in a separate pan—you deserve it!). You can roughly shape the biscuits into 2-inch rounds with your fingers, but be careful not to overwork the dough. Brush cream and sprinkle turbinado sugar over the top of each biscuit.

5. Set a baking sheet on a lower rack of the oven to catch any bubble-overs. Bake until the biscuits are cooked through and golden brown and the juices are thickened and bubbling, 40 to 45 minutes. Serve with vanilla ice cream.

DEEP DISH STRAWBERRY LATTICE PIE

Throughout our 4th of July family get together this year, my kids and niece and nephew piped up several times to check on the status of this pie, "Are we gonna eat the strawberry pie yet?" The bright red gingham-checked pie on the counter tempted them for hours before the time finally came to start slicing. As visually enticing as this deep dish dessert is, the flavors are equally crave worthy, with hints of cinnamon, vanilla, and lemon enhancing the strawberries.

 **Makes 9 servings**

INGREDIENTS:

Crust:

2½ cups all-purpose flour

2 tablespoons sugar

½ teaspoon coarse salt

1¼ cups (2½ sticks) unsalted butter, diced and chilled

4 to 10 tablespoons ice water

1 large egg

4 teaspoons raw turbinado sugar

Filling:

2 pounds fresh strawberries, hulled and halved

½ cup sugar

½ cup firmly packed brown sugar

⅓ cup cornstarch

1 tablespoon freshly squeezed lemon juice

1 tablespoon vanilla extract

1 teaspoon ground cinnamon

DIRECTIONS:

1. To make the crust, briefly pulse the flour, sugar, and salt to combine in a food processor.* Add the cold butter and pulse 5 to 7 times, until you have pea-sized chunks within the mixture. Add in the ice water, 2 tablespoons at a time, and pulse until the mixture is moist enough that when you pinch a bit between your fingers it holds together (you may need more or less water, depending on the humidity in your kitchen). Transfer the mixture to a clean surface, form the dough into two balls (one slightly larger than the other), wrap each with plastic wrap and flatten them into disks. Refrigerate for at least 1 hour.

Continued on next page

There are many ways to make a pie crust—I've found the food processor method to be among the easiest. If you don't have a food processor, you can always prepare the dough in a stand mixer, with a pastry blender, or by hand.

2. **Heat the oven to 400° F.**

3. Stir together the ingredients for the filling in a large bowl.

4. Roll out the larger of the pie dough disks on a lightly floured surface to about a ⅛-inch thickness, in roughly a 13x13-inch square. Carefully transfer the dough to an 8x8-inch ceramic or glass baking dish and gently fit it into place, doing your best not to stretch it. Don't trim the edges. Spoon in the filling.

5. Roll out the remaining pie dough and slice it into eight 1-inch strips (a pizza cutter works well for this). Lay four dough strips, evenly spaced, vertically across the top of the pie. Weave the remaining four dough strips horizontally across the pie to form a lattice pattern. Trim the ends of the strips and fold the edges from the bottom crust over the strips and press to seal.

6. Whisk the egg with a splash of water in a small bowl to make an egg wash. Brush the crust with the egg wash and sprinkle on raw turbinado sugar.

7. Bake until the filling is bubbly (set a baking sheet on a lower rack to catch any spillovers) and the crust is a deep golden brown, 50 to 60 minutes. If the edges start to brown too fast, cover them with foil. Allow the pie to cool to room temperature before serving.

CROISSANT BREAD PUDDING WITH ESPRESSO BUTTERSCOTCH SAUCE

Breakfast was my inspiration for pairing this pillowy croissant bread pudding with espresso butterscotch sauce—just like a croissant and a latte. It has the requisite bread pudding soft custard inside, but on the outside it's all about the crispy, flaky layers of the croissants and the crunch of toasted hazelnuts.

 **Makes 8 servings**

INGREDIENTS:

Croissant Bread Pudding:

6 day-old croissants (about 10 ounces), cut into 1-inch pieces
3 large eggs
2 egg yolks
2 cups whole milk
1 cup heavy cream
1 cup sugar
1 tablespoon vanilla extract
½ teaspoon ground cinnamon
¼ teaspoon coarse salt
¼ cup hazelnuts, roughly chopped

Espresso Butterscotch Sauce:

6 tablespoons unsalted butter
1 cup firmly packed brown sugar
1 cup heavy cream
2 tablespoons light corn syrup
2 tablespoons vanilla extract
2 teaspoons instant espresso powder
Pinch coarse salt

DIRECTIONS:

1. **Heat the oven to 350° F.**

2. Grease an 8x8-inch glass or ceramic baking dish or metal baking pan with butter or baking spray.

Continued on next page

CROISSANT BREAD PUDDING WITH ESPRESSO BUTTERSCOTCH SAUCE—*continued*

MAKE IT A DECAF: If you're going to serve this to kids and you'd rather not have them wired on caffeine, just omit the espresso powder. The homemade butterscotch sauce on its own is still something special.

3. Spread out the croissant pieces on a rimmed baking sheet in a single layer. Toast them in the oven until they're crisp and just beginning to brown, 8 to 10 minutes.

4. Transfer the croissants to the prepared dish or pan. (The bread pudding will look prettier if you arrange the pieces so the cut sides face down and the flaky exterior sides are on top.)

5. In a large bowl, whisk together the eggs, yolks, milk, cream, sugar, vanilla, cinnamon, and salt. Pour the mixture over the croissants, making sure to coat each piece. Some of the croissants may begin to float in the egg mixture—gently press on them to saturate them; they will settle as they absorb the liquid. Cover the dish with foil and refrigerate for 30 minutes.

6. **If you're using a glass or ceramic baking dish, turn down the heat on the oven to 325°F.** Keep the heat at 350°F for metal baking pans.

7. Bake, covered, for 35 minutes. Remove the foil and scatter the hazelnuts over the top. Continue baking, uncovered, until the pudding is puffed, the bread and hazelnuts are toasted on top and a toothpick inserted in the center comes out clean, 30 to 40 minutes more.

Continued on next page

8. While the pudding is baking, prepare the sauce. Melt the butter in a heavy-bottomed medium saucepan over medium heat. Add in the brown sugar, cream, and corn syrup and stir constantly until the mixture comes to a boil. Continue boiling, stirring occasionally, until the syrup is slightly thickened, 5 to 7 minutes. Remove from the heat and whisk in the vanilla, espresso powder and salt. The syrup may seem bit clumpy and separated at this point—don't worry. Set it aside to cool for about 20 minutes and it will thicken further. Whisk it again and it should now come together.

9. Serve the bread pudding warm or at room temperature, with the espresso butterscotch sauce spooned over the top.

WATERMELON-LIME JELLY CUBES

Sure, you can make store-bought gelatin in your 8x8 dish, but why not go for an even better treat and make your own from scratch? Watermelon is naturally bright pink, sweet, and full of water, making it the perfect homemade gelatin flavor. Share these cubes as a refreshing, lighter dessert option for a summertime barbecue.

 **Makes 64 cubes**

INGREDIENTS:

8 to 10 cups cubed seedless watermelon

¾ cup sugar

5 (¼ ounce) packets unflavored gelatin

3 tablespoons freshly squeezed lime juice

⅓ cup chopped fresh mint

DIRECTIONS:

1. Grease an 8x8-inch glass or ceramic baking dish or metal baking pan with oil or cooking spray and wipe out the excess with a paper towel.

2. Puree the watermelon in a food processor or blender. Pour the puree through a fine-mesh sieve into a medium bowl to strain out the pulp—you want a total of 6 cups of strained watermelon juice. Transfer 1 cup of the watermelon juice and the sugar to a small saucepan. Bring the mixture to a boil, stirring until the sugar is dissolved. Transfer another 1 cup of the watermelon juice to a large bowl and sprinkle the gelatin over the surface. Let the gelatin stand for 1 minute. Pour the boiling juice mixture over the gelatin and stir until the gelatin is completely dissolved, 1 to 2 minutes. Stir in the remaining watermelon juice and the lime juice.

Continued on next page

GELATIN FOR GROWN-UPS: If you'd like to take a boozier approach to these cubes, add a few good splashes of tequila or vodka along with the lime juice.

3. Pour the gelatin mixture into the prepared dish or pan. Skim off any foam that may form on the surface with a spoon. Refrigerate the gelatin until it's completely set, at least 4 hours. Cut the gelatin into 1-inch cubes, and garnish each cube with mint. Serve chilled.

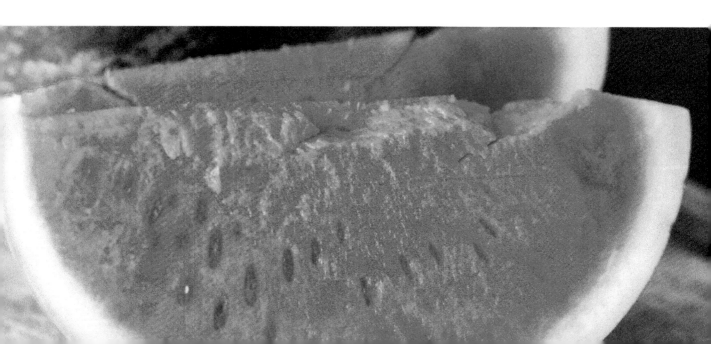

COCONUT RICE PUDDING

I converted two members of my household into rice pudding fans with this baked coconut flavored version. It's aromatic, sweet, and creamy, with a tropical twist. Unlike some rice pudding recipes, which call for pre-cooked rice, the rice here simmers in the milks, slowly becoming one—a delicious marriage, of sorts. I was a little skeptical of this technique from Mark Bittman, which starts with just one-third cup of long-grain rice and calls for diligent stirring at regular intervals, but it turns out to be ingenious.

G C **Makes 4 to 6 servings**

INGREDIENTS:

⅓ cup jasmine rice*

½ cup sugar

Pinch salt

2 cups coconut milk

2 cups whole milk

2 teaspoons vanilla extract

½ cup sweetened shredded coconut

You can substitute another long-grain rice, but I think aromatic jasmine rice tastes best with coconut. It's usually sold alongside other rice varieties at the grocery store, or possibly in the Asian foods aisle.

DIRECTIONS:

1. **Heat the oven to 300° F.**

2. In an 8x8-inch glass or ceramic baking dish, combine the rice, sugar, salt, coconut milk, milk, and vanilla. Bake, uncovered, for 30 minutes. Give it a stir and return it to the oven for another 30 minutes, then stir again. During this segment, the mixture will have bubbled up a bit and a film will form on the surface—just stir it in. Bake for another 30 minutes, and stir again. Start checking and stirring the pudding every 10 minutes from this point—it should be done after about 30 minutes (a grand total of about 2 hours). You'll know it's done when the rice has expanded and the milks have thickened. The pudding will continue to thicken as it cools.

Continued on next page

3. Spread the shredded coconut on a rimmed baking sheet and toast it in the oven until it's lightly browned, 5 to 7 minutes (keep an eye on it, as it can burn quickly). Sprinkle the toasted coconut over the top of the pudding. Serve warm, room temperature, or cold.

MARY'S BEST BAKLAVA

You just can't rush the good stuff. Baklava is one of those desserts that takes time, dedication, and patience to prepare—but the results not only justify your efforts, they inspire you to want to make it all over again to share with more people. This rendition of baklava comes from my friend Eleni's mother, Mary, from Greece and it is crispier and flakier than any other baklava I've ever tasted. It starts in an extra hot oven, then slowly bakes at a low temperature until the delicate phyllo layers fully crisp up, ready to soak in the sweet (and lightly citrusy) syrup.

 Makes 32 pieces

INGREDIENTS:

Baklava:

6 ounces (about 1½ cups) finely
   chopped walnuts
¼ cup dry bread crumbs
¼ cup sugar
1 teaspoon ground cinnamon
⅛ teaspoon salt
13 tablespoons unsalted butter, divided
½ pound frozen phyllo dough, thawed
   to room temperature*

Syrup:

1 cup sugar
½ cup water
1 tablespoon freshly squeezed
   lemon juice
1 cinnamon stick

Phyllo dough is typically sold in 1-pound packages. The easiest thing to do is to thaw the whole package, then cut the stack of dough sheets in half with kitchen shears or a sharp knife. Use one half for this recipe; re-roll and wrap up the remaining half and store it in the refrigerator for up to 10 days for another use, such as the Smoked Salmon, Spinach, and Herbed Goat Cheese Phyllo pie on page 39.

Continued on next page

MARY'S BEST BAKLAVA—*continued*

[KEEP IT COVERED: Working with phyllo can be a bit intimidating due to its tissue paper thin nature and its propensity to dry out. Show phyllo who's boss! In between pulling out sheets, be sure to cover the stack with a piece of plastic wrap and a damp towel. This will help the phyllo retain its moisture and make it much easier to handle.]

DIRECTIONS:

1. **Heat the oven to 500° F.**

2. If you haven't already done so, set out your phyllo dough to come to room temperature.

3. In a medium bowl, combine the walnuts, bread crumbs, sugar, cinnamon, and salt.

4. Melt 8 tablespoons of butter (1 stick) in a microwave-safe bowl in the microwave on high for about 1 minute, or in a small saucepan over medium heat.

5. Unroll the phyllo dough. With kitchen shears or a sharp knife, trim the stack of dough sheets to 8x8-inch squares (use a ruler or your baking pan as a guide). Immediately cover the phyllo with a sheet of plastic wrap and a damp towel so it doesn't dry out—be sure to keep it covered whenever you're not lifting out a new sheet.

Continued on next page

6. Brush melted butter inside the bottom of an 8x8-inch metal baking pan. (IMPORTANT: Do NOT use glass, ceramic baking dishes, or *nonstick* metal pans as they are not recommended for high heat). Layer on four phyllo sheets, brushing each one with butter before adding the next. Sprinkle ½ cup of the walnut mixture over the surface. Layer on three more phyllo sheets, again brushing each one with butter before adding the next. Sprinkle another ½ cup of the walnut mixture over the surface. Repeat the last two layers two more times (you should have used all of your walnut mixture). Layer on five sheets of phyllo, with butter between each, to top the baklava.

7. With a sharp, serrated knife cut the baklava into 32 triangles by first dividing the batch into 16 squares, then bisecting the squares diagonally.

8. Melt the remaining 5 tablespoons of butter in a small saucepan over low heat. Once it's melted it will begin to sputter and foam. Let the foam rise to the top and, once the butter is no longer sputtering, remove the saucepan from the heat and spoon off the foam until the remaining butter is clear. Spoon the clarified butter over the top of the baklava (don't pour it on all at once or the phyllo will become soggy).

9. Set the pan in the oven and immediately turn the temperature down to 250° F. Bake for 2 hours.

10. While the baklava is baking, make the syrup (ideally, you'll want to do this right after you put the baklava in the oven to give it ample time to cool). Combine all of the syrup ingredients in a small saucepan over medium-high heat. Bring the mixture to a boil, stirring until the sugar is dissolved. Continue boiling until the syrup has thickened to a syrup consistency, 3 to 4 minutes. Remove it from the heat and set aside to cool.

11. When the baklava is done baking, and while it is still hot, spoon the cooled syrup over the top. Allow the syrup to soak in for 2 to 3 hours before serving. Baklava is best the day it's made, but it will stay relatively fresh in an airtight container at room temperature for up to 5 days.

Sweet Treats

DULCE DE LECHE

It just might be the easiest caramel sauce ever—and you can bake it right in your 8x8-inch dish with nearly no hands-on effort. *Dulce de leche* (literally "candy made of milk") is popular throughout Latin America for good reason—it is addictively delicious. My favorite way to enjoy this silky, sweet treat is simply drizzled over vanilla ice cream, but you can also stir it into your coffee, spread it on toast, sandwich it between sugar cookies—or just scoop a little up with a spoon.

G C **Makes 1½ cups**

INGREDIENT:

1 (14 ounce) can sweetened condensed milk

DIRECTIONS:

1. **Heat the oven to 425° F.**

2. Pour the milk into an 8x8-inch glass or ceramic baking dish. Cover the dish tightly with foil. Set the dish inside a larger shallow dish (a 13x9-inch dish works well). Fill the larger dish with hot water to a ½-inch depth.

3. Bake for 60 minutes—the milk should have turned a light golden brown. If you prefer a darker dulce de leche you can continue baking, covered, for another 30 minutes. Scrape the milk into a medium bowl and beat with an electric mixer or wooden spoon until smooth. You can use the dulce de leche immediately or transfer to an airtight container for later use. Refrigerate for up to a month.

EASY... AND SAFE! Baking is my preferred method to make dulce de leche, not only because it's so easy and hands-off, but it's also much safer and foolproof than the boil-in-the-can method which can cause an explosion. Yikes!

VANILLA CHAI FUDGE

Look for bagged tea, not chai lattes or other instant mixes.

I learned the merits of infusing tea flavors into my cooking and baking from my friend Annelies Zijderveld, who authored a delightful cookbook called *Steeped: Recipes Infused with Tea*. She describes a myriad of ways to elevate familiar dishes with teas from around the world. Indian masala chai—with its warm notes of cinnamon, cloves, cardamom, ginger, and black tea—gives an aromatic twist to good old-fashioned vanilla fudge.

 **Makes 64 pieces**

INGREDIENTS:

1 tablespoon unsalted butter, plus more for the pan
1 tablespoon vanilla extract
1½ cups heavy cream
5 chai tea bags*

3 cups sugar
¼ cup light corn syrup
¼ teaspoon salt

DIRECTIONS:

1. Line an 8x8-inch glass or ceramic baking dish or metal baking pan with parchment (see page 3 for a tutorial).

2. Place the butter and vanilla in a large bowl and set aside.

3. Heat the cream in a medium saucepan over medium-high heat, stirring occasionally, just until it begins to boil. Remove it from the heat and steep the tea bags in the hot cream for 5 minutes. Discard the tea bags.

Continued on next page

FOLLOW THE DIRECTIONS. NO, REALLY. If there ever was a time to follow recipe directions to the letter, do so when making fudge. There's arguably more science than art to fudge—it's basically one big effort in creating and managing sugar crystals. Heating and cooling to the right temperature is critical to getting a smooth, velvety fudge texture. Grab your thermometer and pay attention to it!

4. Add the sugar, corn syrup, and salt to the cream in the saucepan. Stir over medium heat until the sugar is dissolved. Continue stirring, raise the temperature to medium high, and bring the mixture to a boil. Once it's boiling, stop stirring and attach a candy thermometer to the saucepan. Continue boiling until the thermometer reaches 238° F (soft ball stage). Immediately remove the pan from heat and pour the mixture over the butter and vanilla in the large bowl. **Don't scrape the pan, and don't stir it once you've poured it into the bowl**—doing so may create large crystals, which means a grainy texture. Attach the thermometer to the bowl and allow the mixture to cool, undisturbed, until it falls to 110° F.

5. Remove the thermometer. Beat the mixture with a wooden spoon until it becomes thick and just begins to lose its gloss, about 5 minutes. Pour it into the prepared dish or pan (work quickly, it starts to set pretty fast), spread evenly, and allow the fudge to completely cool and set at room temperature. Once it's completely cooled, you may find it easier to cut the fudge into squares if you set it in the refrigerator for a while. Lift the fudge out of the pan by the parchment paper and cut into 1-inch squares. Fudge should stay fresh at room temperature in an airtight container for up to 2 weeks.

NOTES

MEASUREMENTS EQUIVALENTS

LIQUIDS BY VOLUME

US	Cups	Ounces	Metric*
1/4 tsp			1 ml
1/2 tsp			2 ml
1 tsp			5 ml
3 tsp (1 tbsp)		1/2 fl oz	15 ml
2 tbsp	1/8 cup	1 fl oz	30 ml
4 tbsp	1/4 cup	2 fl oz	60 ml
5 1/3 tbsp	1/3 cup	3 fl oz	80 ml
8 tbsp	1/2 cup	4 fl oz	120 ml
10 2/3 tbsp	2/3 cup	5 fl oz	160 ml
12 tbsp	3/4 cup	6 fl oz	180 ml
16 tbsp	1 cup	8 fl oz	240 ml
1 pint	2 cups	16 fl oz	475 ml
1 quart	4 cups	32 fl oz	945 ml

All conversions are approximate.
*1,000 ml is 1 liter.

DRY INGREDIENTS BY WEIGHT

US/UK	Metric
1/4 oz	7 g
1/2 oz	14 g
1 oz	28 g
2 oz	57 g
3 oz	85 g
4 oz (1/4 lb)	113 g
5 oz	142 g
6 oz	170 g
7 oz	200 g
8 oz (1/2 lb)	227 g
9 oz	255 g
10 oz	284 g
11 oz	312 g
12 oz (3/4 lb)	340 g
13 oz	369 g
14 oz	400 g
15 oz	425 g
16 oz (1 lb)	454 g

OVEN TEMPERATURES

°F	°C	Gas Mark
250	120	1/2
275	140	1
300	150	2
325	165	3
350	180	4
375	190	5
400	200	6
425	220	7
450	230	8
475	245	9
500	260	10
550	290	Broil

ACKNOWLEDGMENTS

It gives me immense pride to thank the many friends, family members and supporters who have taken part in making *The 8x8 Cookbook* happen. Their support, expertise, opinions, and votes of confidence have meant everything to me.

There are definitely perks to having a spouse writing a cookbook—such as a perpetual buffet in the fridge—but it also has its challenges. My husband Mike has been steadfastly supportive of me, he's unabashedly proud of my work, and I quite simply would not have had the space to pursue my entrepreneurial endeavors without him. Thank you so much for all you do for our family and for me. Love you more!

Our kids have watched me blog about food since they were born and they've now observed the cookbook writing process—twice! They see me work hard, but they also see me enjoy what I do. It's an example I'm proud to set, and they inspire me in more ways than they know.

I come from a family of people who "make things", so when I get fired up about an idea like a cookbook or a publishing company, they get it. My sister Angela has been my honest sounding board throughout this project, sharing in my excitement when I'm onto something good and also pumping the brakes (ahem) when I get off track. She, my sister Julie and my mom and dad all tested and tasted numerous recipes and helped me think through decisions every step of the way.

Thanks to Lorna Nakell and Poppy Milliken of Interrobang Collective for patiently and painstakingly designing this beautiful book from cover to cover, editing, and guiding me through the publishing process. We had a lot to do in a short amount of time, and I am so proud of what we accomplished.

I'm so grateful to Jodie Chase of Chase, Ink. Public Relations for all of her publicity efforts and for our daily brainstorm sessions.

Thanks to Meilee Epler for listening to my early plans for this book and immediately jumping on board to help me flesh out my ideas, keep me on track and join me for vintage 8x8 dish shopping excursions.

A small army of recipe testers—longtime friends, brand new friends, friends of friends, friends' mothers, blog readers—gave feedback on each recipe in this book. Each time I learned something valuable to incorporate into the recipe and make it clearer, easier or tastier. This book is better because of Sarah and Ben Aslan, Julie Atkinson, Larissa Baker, Tamara Berg, Melissa Black, Kelly Castellon, Jen Czaja, Lauren Hall, Jenni Harris, Libby Hellmann, Lauren Holiday, Sandra Hoyle, Audrey Jastrow, Tricia Kenny, Michelle Kusanovich, Angela Lipscomb, Nancy Lipscomb, Eleni Mavromati, Kerily McEvoy, Kirsten Medeiros, Alissa Meltzer, Jen Miller, Lisa Muroya, Sarah Orellana, Holly Osment, Amanda Richard, Brooke Russell, Kim Samek, Heather Sblendorio, Sara Scott, Lynne Steele, Colleen Strahs, Susan Strahs, Brenda Thompson, Laura Thompson, Jim Twiss, Lana Walsh, Kelly Williams, Kitty Wilson and Whit Wilson.

I launched The 8x8 Cookbook and Burnt Cheese Press via a successful crowd-funding campaign on Kickstarter. It was one of the most challenging efforts I've ever undertaken, but I was boosted by the sage advice of my friends Nancy Yen and Karen Kart, who generously shared their insights with me.

I'd like to give a special shout-out to my supportive friends who generously helped spread the word about my Kickstarter campaign for this book via their blogs: Liren Baker (KitchenConfidante.com), Karly Campbell (BunsInMyOven.com), Julie Deily (TheLittleKitchen.net), Jenny Flake (PickyPalate.com), Amy Flanigan (VeryCulinary.com), Rachel Gurk (RachelCooks.com), Julie Hession (PeanutButterAndJulie.com), Jane Maynard (ThisWeekForDinner.com), Joanne Ozug (FifteenSpatulas.com), Amanda Rettke (IAmBaker.net), and Gerry Speirs (FoodnessGracious.com).

Thanks to Joe Stoltz of Stoltz Media for creating a top-notch Kickstarter video for the project, from the planning stages to the final presentation. And I thank Tabitha and Dan Jacobson for allowing us to shoot for hours in their kitchen and for setting such a beautiful table.

The success of my Kickstarter campaign would not have been possible without the generosity of the more than 400 amazing supporters who backed the project. I'd like to give special recognition and thanks to those who pledged $100 or more: Sarah Alyea, Felice Arredondo and Tim Salber, The Atkinson Family, Elise Bauer, Casey Benedict, Wendy Bergh, Indie Berkes, Paul Bignardi and Terri Dien, Dan and Stephanie Bryson, Jenn Buechel, Belinda Chan, Jodie Chase, Ellen de Coninck and Simon Whetzel, The Daly Family, Earlene Davis, The Downey Twiss Family, The Froemling Family, Susan Gaffney-Evans, Kathy A.N. Grant, Liz Grant, Jared Hawk, The Idemoto Family, Bryant Jenkins, Kristin B. Jones and McKinley Jones, Jr., Amy Koo, Robin M. Kull, Sarah Lamoree, Madeline J. Ling, DeEdra and Eugene Lipscomb, Amy Littleton, Joanna Salgado Liwanag, Kathleen Luz, Eleni Mavromati, Karen Meade, Alissa and Jonathan Meltzer, Jacqueline and Bob Micera, Lisa Gay Miller, Millie, The Newby Family, Juli Oh, Christine Okubo, The Osment Family, Tammira Philippe, Rick and Becky Smith, Lisa Stone, Colleen and Andrew Strahs, Elizabeth Taylor, Horacio Trujillo, The Vangelis Family, The Vannoni Family, Carin Walden, Sarah Welch, and Karen and Kurt Wolf.

Last, but absolutely not least, I am honored to recognize and thank the inaugural members of the Burnt Cheese Press Founder's Table for their notable support of *The 8x8 Cookbook* and future projects: Betsy Sivage Clark, Evan Klein, Angela Lipscomb and Aldo Davila, Nancy and James Lipscomb, and Ken and Susan Strahs.

INDEX

INDEX

INDEX—*continued*

INDEX—*continued*

CPSIA information can be obtained
at www.ICGtesting.com
Printed in the USA
LVOW05s0443170816

500617LV00054B/240/P